The Happy Palmist

The Happy Palmist

*My Joyful Adventure in
Vedic Palmistry*

Guylaine Vallée and Steve Erwin

Galaxy Publications & Recordings

All rights reserved. No part of this work may be reproduced or used in any form or by any means, graphic, electronic or mechanical, including photocopying, recording, or by any information storage and retrieval system, without the prior written permission of the publisher.

Galaxy Publications & Recordings
576 Route 315, Chénéville, Qc, Canada J0V 1E0
Tel.: 819-428-4298 Fax: 819-428-4494; www.birla.ca

Galaxy Publications & Recordings is a division of the Birla Vedic Network.

Cover artwork: Philippe Couturier-Michaud
Text design and layout: Pauline Edward
Photo on the cover page: Jasmin Mori
Inside photos courtesy of the author

Bibliothèque et Archives nationales du Québec and Library and Archives Canada cataloguing in publication

Vallée, Guylaine, 1959-

    The happy palmist : my joyful adventure in vedic palmistry

    ISBN 978-0-9878999-4-1

    1. Vallée, Guylaine, 1959- . 2. Palmistry. 3. Palmists - Québec (Province) - Biography. I. Erwin, Steve, 1959- . II. Title.

BF940.V34A3 2015b   133.6092 C2015-942546-8

For my beloved teachers Ghanshyam and Kathy, who made this adventure possible.

Contents

Foreword ix
Introduction 1
1. My Family Tree 5
2. Rich in Love 12
3. Into the Dark 19
4. Higher Education 27
5. Paris, City of Lights and Hope 33
6. The Man in the Golden Slippers 41
7. True Calling 48
8. Finding My Center 58
9. My Teachers 65
10. Paramahansa Yogananda 77
11. Family Spirit 82
12. The Art of Palmistry 91
13. The Hands of a Saint 105
14. Into the Heart of India 115
15. Dreams and Disaster 126
16. Staying Strong and Carrying On 136
17. In the Sunshine State 150
18. There's No Place Like Home 162
Acknowledgments 173

Foreword

*E*ACH LIFE IS ROOTED in the soil of personal experience. Our families, education, childhood dreams and first independent choices made during adolescence are the seeds sown in the garden where we seek fulfillment as adults. That garden is unpredictable and can grow in wild and unexpected ways, entangling us in complexity or leaving us lost in shadow. But no matter how confused or dark our past, when we listen to what life is whispering to us, a path emerges, things become brighter and suddenly we find we have come face to face with our destiny.

How often have we heard someone admit that they stumbled upon their true calling accidentally, that an odd choice or unexpected circumstance turned out to be the "right choice" or the "ideal circumstance" that shifted their life in an entirely new direction—the direction they seemed born to follow?

This is what happened to Guylaine Vallée. Coming from a humble background, Guylaine first struggled to find happiness by achieving the dreams of her youth: becoming an actress and singer, working in television, traveling, writing. For years, she searched for something that would move her deeply, bring joy to her spirit and assure her she was accomplishing whatever it was she had been put on Earth to do. But each new endeavor and career success led her only from disappointment to disenchantment. None of her accomplishments brought her happiness because none touched her true heart's desire. What Guylaine really wanted to be "when she grew up" was something she had innately known as a young girl—something she had always known and something she had even once proclaimed in front of her entire third-grade class: "I want to be a good person!"

As we all know, destiny has a way of catching up with us. It caught up with Guylaine the day a friend casually mentioned the name Ghanshyam Singh Birla, a Vedic palmist from India living in Montreal. Ghanshyam was a complete stranger to Guylaine, but his name resonated so strongly with her that she knew she had to meet him—life was whispering to her, and she listened.

In her compelling memoir, *The Happy Palmist: My Joyful Adventure in Vedic Palmistry*, Guylaine recounts her first remarkable encounter with Ghanshyam, on May 4, 1984. On that day, she knows her life has just taken a major turn and that what she has so long been looking for has finally been revealed to her. She discovers her *life mission*—to help others become better human beings and realize their full potential. Guylaine recognizes that palmistry, a method to understand human behavior, is deeply spiritual, and this is in perfect harmony with her inner quest. The little girl who wanted to "be a good person" finally hears an echo of her deepest desire.

Despite its bright promise, the new direction Guylaine dedicates her life to is demanding, often painfully so. In order to gain the knowledge necessary to become an effective palmist herself, she must examine the depths of her heart and psyche, stripping away all pretense, ego and self-delusion until her soul is bared and she encounters the naked truth about herself.

It is an amazing journey on which she is magnificently guided by Ghanshyam, who encourages her to meditate, practice Kriya Yoga and study the texts that illuminate the ancient Kriya Yoga's teachings, including the masterful classic *Autobiography of a Yogi* by Paramahansa Yogananda. As she grows both spiritually and as a palmist, Guylaine discovers every person we meet in life is our teacher, and every ordinary, daily event can instruct us on how to live a more spiritual existence. Guylaine is accompanied on this incredible adventure by her new colleagues and friends, who are also seeking to become their best possible selves through the study of Kriya Yoga and palmistry and who become her teachers and family.

Early in her studies she discovers that handprints reveal both our past and present and can guide us toward a rewarding future, that the hands are precious instruments of transformation. She learns that the lines of the palm are not fixed, as is commonly believed, but change as we change our thoughts, attitudes and behavior—that they possess a map of our destiny, which we can control, making any future we envision a possibility!

This is far from the notion most have of the nature of palmistry. Indeed, one can believe—as I once did—that the predictions of palmistry are rigid and unchanging and that a palmist will simply tell us what our future holds in store for us: whether we will have children, enjoy good health, or suffer failures or prosper, or whether our love life will be stable or tumultuous.

When I consulted Guylaine for the first time, I did not know what to expect. I was almost afraid of what I would discover, believing my destiny was immutable in my handprints. Fatalism not being part of my vision of the world and human beings, I was fearful of what Guylaine was going to say!

As a writer, language itself and human behavior are my main source of material and I am always striving to increase my knowledge and understanding of myself, of life in all its beauty and complexity, and of the things that connect us to others and to the world in which we live. My whole approach is based on our ability to transform ourselves—that we possess the power to change our lives no matter what hand we were dealt at birth. My books question existence and deal with how difficulties and stressful events can become wonderful opportunities for *recommencements*, an invitation to create new paths for ourselves that will allow us to continue to grow and flourish.

I did not seek out Guylaine to solve a particular problem, to find answers or to give my life a new direction. My personal journey has led me to experiment with various tools and methods of self-knowledge. Like many artists and public figures who have visited Guylaine over the years, my interest in palmistry was based on a desire to cast what I thought I knew about myself in a different light. I wanted to shift my point of view, to find a method of furthering my inner evolution and deepen my spiritual journey.

My first visit did not disappoint me! I came away with a new astrological sign that modified and clarified the way I saw myself. And, most importantly, Guylaine had not *predicted* anything to me, she had not addressed any aspect of my life fatalistically. Far from her revealing my future to me, she revealed truths about myself and suggested ways *I* could direct my life and energies so that I could realize my full potential! Instead of prediction, there was choice—the choice to see the palms of the hands for what they are—mirrors of the self and windows to the soul. In learning to read what those mirrors have to tell us, we learn a way to cope with the changes life thrusts upon us that force us to grow and fulfill our destiny.

Far from prophesizing or offering revelation of a future cast in stone, the lines of our hands reveal our past—and understanding our past is essential to understanding and changing our present. Moreover, the lines of our hands have the ability to transform us, and we will witness them transform as we ourselves evolve. There is a continual and powerful dialogue between our hands and our heart that contains a wealth of information on how to change our lives for the better—Vedic palmistry and its sister science, Vedic astrology, provide us with the language necessary to comprehend and benefit from that dialogue.

To help others transform their lives, we must first follow the demanding path of self-realization ourselves. We must learn to walk in this life with devotion and unconditional love, to be capable of compassion and of offering our hearts to others with an unshakable faith that every human being has the ability to create a better life, to grow spiritually and to experience joy. To inspire others to change, we must be in constant positive movement—ceaselessly seeking to know ourselves and the nature of human behavior. Guylaine embodies that quality.

The book you hold in your hands is a rich, honest and inspiring tale of a passionate young woman's spiritual journey exploring the ancient roots of Vedic palmistry. Through this tale, we are introduced to the warmth and wisdom of Guylaine's remarkable spiritual guide, Ghanshyam Singh Birla, who steers Guylaine along the road that leads to self-knowledge. After reading Guylaine's story you will have no doubt that we can and must rely on ourselves to fulfill our dreams and find fulfillment in life, and that an essential part of our happiness rests in the palm of our hands!

Hélène Dorion
Author of *Recommencements*
Officer of the Order of Canada
Knight of the National Order of Quebec

Introduction

Lines to Live By

THE BLAZING CALCUTTA SUN beat down on us as I rushed alongside Mother Teresa, trying my best to keep up with the elderly nun. She was twice my age but had three times my energy, and she was in a hurry. Afternoon prayers were about to start and she was passing out medallions of the Blessed Mother to dozens of people who had come from around the world to see her; they were lined up eagerly waiting to receive her blessing.

"Don't fall behind, dear," she encouraged me as we moved down the line, placing medallions in outstretched hands. Many had tears of joy in their eyes; I understood their elation. I had admired Mother Teresa's selflessness and devotion to others since childhood and had come to see her at her Missionaries of Charity in 1996 on a mission of my own—I wanted her handprints.

"No one has ever asked me for that before," she said, shaking her head. "I'm sorry, I just don't have time."

"I understand, Mother, I only ask because I believe seeing your hands would help others … my students could learn a lot …"

I am not sure she heard what I was saying, but she stopped and turned to look at me with her dark, penetrating eyes, then held out her hands with her palms facing up.

"What is it you want to see in these old hands?"

I wanted to see everything, and I did. The lines and signs crisscrossing her strong, beautiful palms revealed a lifetime of service to others, a deep compassion for humanity and a choice made at an early age to abandon ego and follow a spiritual path of love and humility toward God—none of which surprised me.

Our hands are a reflection of who we are, and seeing Mother Teresa's palms was a dramatic confirmation of what I had known for many years—our hands never lie. They are windows into our soul, a record of who we are—our past and present deeds and desires, hopes and fears, flaws and potential all etched in the lines of our palm.

But our lines are not our fate. The wonderful thing about the lines of our hands is that we can change them if we want to—as we change our thoughts, attitudes and actions, our lines will mirror that change. That is what makes palmistry—a powerful method of self-knowledge that stretches back to the beginning of civilization—such an amazing tool for personal growth and transformation.

If we allow them, our hands can help us shape our future and guide us to a life of purpose, happiness, health and joy! That is not a prediction, it is a fact—and I speak from personal experience.

I have been practicing *hast jyotish*—the ancient science of Vedic palmistry—for 30 years (I can't believe it has been that long!). I have studied the handprints of thousands of people from every walk of life—child prodigies, murderers, farmers, scientists, rock stars—even a living saint. But the hands I have learned the most from are my own.

When I was in my 20s, I should have been on top of the world. I came from a loving family, had a good education, was young and pretty, and was living in Paris—the most romantic city in the world. I had a glamorous job in television and an expense account that allowed me to shop in the city's finest boutiques.

And yet, I was miserable and had been for years. But I did not know why. My life lacked meaning and purpose no matter what I did or where I traveled. Sadness seemed to be my destiny.

Then, one single consultation with a remarkable Vedic palmist changed the way I viewed myself and the world. I saw all my fears, anxieties and a dozen other "spiritual blockages" staring up at me in the lines of my hands—everything that had kept me from happiness. Once I knew what they were, I was able to set about removing them.

Since that day, I have been on a journey of self-discovery, a journey that has lifted me from the depths of despair and delivered me to a place of peace and true happiness.

I may not have the saintly lines of Mother Teresa, but the study of palmistry has exposed me to the words and wisdom of a hundred saints and sages whom I carry in my heart whenever I sit down to do a reading or teach a class on the heart line.

Palmistry has brought love and joy into my life, and it is my deepest wish that it could do the same for you. If nothing else, I hope my story will inspire you to look at your hands a little differently.

CHAPTER 1

My Family Tree

MY FIRST MEMORY IS a moment of perfect happiness. I was two years old and sitting at the tiny kitchen table in the playhouse my father had built for me in our backyard in Lancaster, Ontario. I don't remember what I was doing, but I recall the feeling—complete contentment, bliss. The playhouse was a gift from my dad, who loved two things—his family and working with his hands. When he combined his two passions, he made magic happen. And my little house was truly magical. Dad designed every detail so I would feel I belonged there, from the miniature cupboards, to the tiny table and chairs and the little cradle that held my doll. He created a world just for me, to make me feel special and so I would know I was exactly where I was supposed to be, and that was perfect happiness.

Many years later I would set out on a journey to rediscover that sense of connectedness and peace, a journey that would take me down dark paths, introduce me to beautiful friends and eventually lead me to my life's true passion and purpose—palmistry, and the great truths and life changing wisdom that ancient, elegant science has to offer us all.

I was born in Lancaster on the second day of spring in 1959, but I did not live there long enough to really call it home. My parents, Lionel and Laurette Vallée, grew up in Quebec and had moved to the Ontario town temporarily because Dad needed a job to feed his kids (four boys and two girls), of which I was the youngest and most doted on. Neither my mom nor my dad spoke

English, and when I was three years old and Dad's job ended, so did our time in Lancaster. My folks loaded the kids and everything we owned into the family Buick—except my little house because it was too big—and we headed for Quebec.

My parents did not have much money when we were growing up. They worked hard to provide for us and made a lot of sacrifices, often living apart for long stretches whenever Dad, a carpenter by training, was forced to work out of town. It was tough on them because they loved each other so much, but they showered us with affection and made sure we had what was most important. Mom used to say, "We may be poor, but we're rich in love." No matter how difficult things were, Mom and Dad never complained about their lives, made us feel safe and secure, and always put family first—values they had learned from their own parents.

Dad, the fourth of 11 children, was born in the spring of 1920 in the small, rural parish of Saint-Gédéon-de-Beauce, about 140 kilometers south of Quebec City. My paternal grandfather, Nazaire Vallée, owned a farm, but also worked sculpting granite tombstones to make ends meet. He never expected that one day he would carve his wife's name onto one of those stones. Dad's mom, Albertine, died suddenly from an inflamed thyroid gland at the young age of 46, when my dad was still a boy. It was a terrible shock to the family. His sisters did their best to fill in for their mother, taking on the daily chores and running the household, but money was tight and Dad stepped up to help support the family. Although he had barely learned to read and write, he quit school, worked at any job he could find, and became an accomplished farmer, carpenter and lumberjack. He walked or hitchhiked to nearby lumber camps, swung an axe from sunrise to sundown to put a few extra pennies into his father's hands, and earned a reputation as an honorable and hardworking family man.

When I was a kid, I would imagine what he had been doing at my age. Sometimes I would tell him how much I admired what he had done for his family, but he would shrug and say, "I'm just happy I was able to help out when help was needed."

Dad's early life was hard and lonely, but that changed the day he first looked into the beautiful blue eyes of Laurette Couture. Although Mom grew up in the neighboring village of Saint-Martin-de-Beauce, they did not meet until they were adults.

Mom's family was even bigger than Dad's. Born in 1924, she was the youngest of 14 children. According to family lore, Grandpa Xavier Couture and his 13 kids were picking strawberries when Grandma Alphonsine went into labor with my mom. By the time Grandpa returned with the berries, his new daughter was already in the cradle waiting for him. Alphonsine was a very busy bee, keeping track of more than a dozen children, preparing enough hot meals each day to feed a small army—growing her own vegetables, churning her own butter and preserving jams. She was a skilled seamstress and dressed the entire family with her own creations.

Both Grandpa and Grandma Couture had generous hearts. Whenever a neighbor passed away, Grandpa built a coffin to donate to the grieving family and Alphonsine lined it with silk. One day, Grandpa made a coffin for a young boy, and my mom, who was just three, crawled inside to play with her doll. Thank goodness Grandma found her before the casket was delivered!

Like me, Mom was the baby of the family and, like me, she was left-handed. On her first day of school, she came home with bruises across her fingers and told her worried mother that the teacher had hit her with a ruler because she was writing with her left hand. When Grandpa got wind of this, he stormed down to the school and confronted the teacher, who said it was school policy to discipline left-handed children and force them to use their right hands at all times.

"I don't give a damn," Grandpa said, snatching her ruler and snapping it in half. "If you ever harm my little girl, or any child, I'll make sure you never teach again."

Grandpa sat on the school board and the shaken teacher knew he could make good on his threat; she never hit my mother again. But the damage had been done to little left-handed Laurette—it had been beaten into her that it was better to be right-handed. She got used to writing with her right hand at school, but at home she fumbled whenever she used a pair of scissors or drew a picture, something she enjoyed immensely.

"Don't worry about that teacher," Grandma would soothe her. "You must always be true to yourself and never try to be what someone else wants you to be. Have fun my beautiful girl, you are very talented! Use your left hand."

From that day forward, Mom used her left hand to draw and it became clear her creativity was expressed through that hand. She took up painting later in life and became a gifted and prolific artist. Many of Mom's beautiful acrylics and watercolors hang proudly on the walls of my home today and I treasure them dearly.

Despite the painful experience with her first teacher, Mom loved school. She was extremely sociable and such a good student that, when she was just 14, the school director offered her the opportunity to travel to the city to train as a teacher. However, she was the beloved baby of the family and my grandparents said they would miss her too much if she left, and so they did not let her go.

My mom seldom complained about anything, but she confided in me that she would have loved to become a teacher. I have no doubt she would have been an exceptional one, and I am certain I inherited my own love of teaching from her.

When Mom left school in 1939, at the age of 15, Grandpa Xavier, who was managing a lumberjack camp, hired her and her sister Rose-Aimée to run the camp kitchen during the frigid winter. For four months, they catered to 50 rough-and-tumble lumberjacks, rising two hours before dawn every morning to load firewood into the ovens and prepare mountain-high stacks of pancakes and massive pots of porridge and beans. In the evening, it was vats of soup and stew, meat and potatoes and two dozen freshly baked pies for dessert. Then they would prep for the next day, clean up the kitchen and collapse onto their cots.

Long before my parents met, Mom had heard about the young Vallée boy who had lost his mother at a young age and worked hard to help his family. She was moved by his determination and dedication. When they were eventually introduced by a mutual friend, Mom, who had just turned 18, looked straight into Dad's heart and knew he was the one.

"I loved your father from the moment I saw him," she told me.

My 22-year-old dad felt the same way, and grew tongue-tied in front of the beautiful Laurette, with her curly black hair and sparkling sapphire eyes. But he mustered up the nerve to ask if he could call on her and was surprised and delighted when she replied with an immediate *yes*.

The courtship was old-fashioned and romantic—their dates were chaperoned and they communicated through love letters— far more intimate than the telephone, considering every line in town was shared by several families. When they visited the sugar shack to sample maple syrup, Dad carved Mom her own wooden spoon so she would not have to share it with anyone else.

They married in 1944, two years after they had met, in a double ceremony with Mom's sister Rose-Aimée and her fiancé, Ovila. Grandpa Xavier built them a bedroom set as a wedding gift and, because Dad had rented a small farm, Grandpa also gave them a cow. A few months later, Mom and Dad became the proud parents of a baby calf.

A few weeks shy of their first wedding anniversary, they were blessed with their first child—my eldest brother, Réjean, who had curly black hair just like my mother. Mom used to say that every new mother would be lucky to have such a sweet and quiet first child. It was a good thing Réjean let Mom get her rest, because life was about to get very hectic for the Vallée family.

By the time Réjean was born, my parents knew they did not want to be farmers; they wanted to raise kids, not crops. So Dad took a gamble—he left the farm and moved his wife and baby to Magog, Quebec, where he had been offered a job at the town's cotton mill. They lived in a spare room in the home of one of Dad's sisters and Mom babysat her kids in exchange for the use of their automatic washing machine—quite a luxury in those days! Dad worked long shifts at the mill and attended night school to earn his carpentry certification. Over the next three years, they welcomed two more sons into the family—first Gaston, then Marcel. Mom was great with budgeting and they saved enough money to allow Dad to build his first house, which he finished in time for the arrival of my brother André in 1952 and my sister Micheline (Mimi) three years later.

My parents could not have been happier. Money was tight, but they had a big family, a new house filled with love and healthy kids.

But then Dad was laid off from the mill and could not find work anywhere nearby. Eventually, a friend helped him get a job in Lancaster. And even though he did not speak a word of English and could not bear to part with his wife and kids, Dad had no choice but to take the offer and move to Ontario, leaving Mom on her own to look after the entire family. As always, Mom managed. But she had to be even more frugal and clever with money. She made all the kids' clothes herself, like her mother before her; when she could not afford to buy new buttons, she would cut them off the winter outfits and sew them onto the summer ones when the season changed. Mom was coping, until the day a neighbor pounded on the front door.

"Laurette, Laurette! Hurry! Come quickly!" he shouted. "Your son Gaston collapsed in school!"

Mom plopped Mimi in her stroller, raced to the school and got Gaston home and into bed. His joints ached and he had a terrible headache. He was throwing up nonstop and continued to retch through the night. There had been a recent polio outbreak and Mom was terrified he had contracted the dreaded disease. She administered the age-old remedy of a shot of gin in a cup of hot water, then called the doctor, who, to my mother's relief, said, "He has symptoms of polio, but I think it's just a bad stomach flu and the gin might have already killed the bug." Gaston's health seemed to improve, but within a few days Mom noticed he was limping. The limp worsened with each passing day. She took him to see more doctors, but none of them could say for certain what was wrong with him.

Gaston's condition deteriorated and, for the first time in her life, my mother felt overwhelmed. Not only did she have a sick child and four healthy ones to care for, she discovered that she was pregnant again—this time with me. It was too much for her to bear alone. She rented out the home Dad had built, packed up the kids and, without a word of English and only a couple of dollars in her purse, she headed west to Ontario to join my father.

CHAPTER 2

Rich in Love

I WAS BORN WITH A flair for the dramatic, making my grand entrance into this life at 2 p.m. on March 22, 1959. It happened so quickly that Mom did not have time to make it to the hospital. Luckily, it was a Sunday, so Dad was home and able to run for the nurse who lived up the street. A few minutes after they arrived, there I was—a healthy, redheaded, eight-pound baby girl.

The delivery went smoothly, but when Dad walked the nurse home, he left the bedroom door ajar and my brother Gaston's cat slipped into the room. The cat jumped into my crib, throwing my mother into a panic—she snatched me from the crib, chased the cat away and held me in her arms under the blankets to protect me until my father returned. The excitement and exertion caused Mom to hemorrhage and Dad had to run back for the nurse. Mom and I were fine, but that was it for Gaston's cat—out he went.

Poor Gaston—it turned out he had a rare but treatable bone disease and had to undergo major surgery to straighten his legs and repair his limp. The operation was a success, but for the next two years he wore casts on both legs that ran from his heels to his hips. He could not walk and was virtually housebound between the ages of 11 and 13. My parents had gotten the cat to keep him occupied while he recovered—once the cat was gone, I became my brother's new entertainment. For the next year and a half, Gaston changed my diapers, bathed me, gave me my bottle and rocked me to sleep. He was an excellent babysitter, which was a big help for my mom, who was busy caring for him and the rest of us. At night, my four-year-old sister Mimi would crawl into bed and sleep next to me as though I were her dolly—I was the baby of the family and everybody wanted a turn with me.

Living in Lancaster was good for the family—Dad was working hard six days a week, but at least we were all together. Dad was a prankster and was always playing tricks on the boys. Despite his money worries and the long hours he worked, he was always cheerful, and his happy whistling and laughter filled the house. My brothers made friends at school, played a lot of sports and learned to speak English; Mom kept busy managing our new home, watching over Mimi and me, sewing our clothes and making sure Gaston kept his strength up. In the winter, she organized family hockey games—Gaston was propped up in front of the goalie net and Mom and the boys would skate around him trying to score. When the weather was warm and I was old enough to walk, I would play in the little house Dad had built for me in the backyard.

It was a picture-perfect family portrait, but our sojourn in Ontario was cut short when Dad was laid off again. Fortunately, my father had a lot of friends who would help him find work. One of them got him a new job in Valleyfield, Quebec, a small town 30 minutes southwest of Montreal on a peninsula bordering Lake St. Francis, famous for its annual speedboat races.

Mom and Dad wanted to build us a permanent home of our own, but they needed to save money to buy property, so our first few years in Valleyfield turned out to be very cozy. The eight of us—Mom, Dad and the six of us kids—squeezed into a small two-bedroom apartment. My parents had one bedroom, my four brothers shared the other, and Mimi and I slept on a foldout couch in the living room. The living room was a hub of activity when my bedtime rolled around, so every night I would go to sleep in my parents' bed and when things quieted down Mom or Dad carried me to the couch and tucked me in beside my sister. I loved to sleep in when I was a kid, and I usually slept later than everyone else. I would wake up to the sound of the boys bouncing around getting ready for school, Dad whistling as he headed off to work and Mom banging pots and pans in the kitchen. I loved the commotion and the close quarters. My brothers would bring their pals over to hang out and Réjean would break out his guitar and ask me to dance for everybody. I drank up the attention.

One day, Dad came home with some big news—he had found an empty plot of land that was the ideal place to build a home—it literally had our name written all over it.

"It's on Vallée Street! Could there be a more perfect place for the Vallée family to live? The Vallées of Vallée Street in Valleyfield!"

Dad worked on the house every weekend with Réjean—who was 19 by then and studying to become an electrician. A few years later, Réjean was wiring homes throughout the area and eventually opened his own electrical company in Valleyfield. Our house went up in no time, although Dad spent years finishing the interior—he was a perfectionist and he loved carpentry.

The new house was my first real home, and it was magnificent. There were plenty of bedrooms for everyone, a big living room for company and parties, a huge basement to play in and an enormous backyard with a stone fire pit that became the go-to location for family and neighborhood barbecues.

My brothers were much older than me—Réjean and I are 14 years apart—and when they (and my many cousins) started getting engaged and married, I was elected to the position of official ring bearer for the extended Vallée-Couture clan and entrusted to carry the precious wedding bands. I loved it—Mom would do up my hair and I got to wear pretty dresses and stay up late drinking 7 Up. As wedding presents, Dad helped the boys build their first homes.

Réjean and I resembled Mom's side of the family and, of all the siblings, we looked the most alike. But our personalities were very different—I was a fun-loving, rambunctious kid and he was very serious and always behaved responsibly. He was a man of few words, but when he spoke, people listened. I was shy around him, but I admired him greatly, as did most people in town—so much so much that one year he was elected commodore of the annual speedboat regatta, which was a very big deal in Valleyfield. The speedboat races still draw thousands of enthusiasts to Valleyfield every summer, doubling the size of the population and pumping hundreds of thousands of dollars into the local economy.

Unlike Réjean, Gaston, the second eldest, was a man of *many* words. He was always the life of the party, a born storyteller, and he could talk for hours about anything. After changing my diapers as a baby, Gaston never shook the habit of looking out for me. He was 12 years older than I and, after becoming an accountant, he worked as the bookkeeper at my high school. One day I decided to skip class and hang out in the lounge with a friend, until an announcement came over the intercom: "Attention students, would Guylaine Vallée please report immediately to the office of Mr. Gaston Vallée." When I got to his office, he shook his head at me. "What do you think you're doing, young lady? Go to your class—now!" It was the last class I ever skipped—too embarrassing!

My brother Marcel was the shyest of the boys, and he had a huge, generous heart. It seemed to me that whenever he threw a party at the house, half of Valleyfield showed up—he had such a happy disposition that people crowded around him to be his friend. Money never seemed to interest him and he once told me, "My only ambition in life is to be happy."

André, Mimi and I were the youngest and closest enough in age to form our own group at the dinner table—there were the three older boys on one side and the three of us on the other. André was full of madcap energy as a teenager and inherited Dad's prankster genes. Once, when he was 12 years old and clowning around at the back of the school bus, he accidently knocked the emergency door open and tumbled out onto the road. Another time, he landed in the hospital when, while helping a friend fix a roof, he stood up to tell a joke and fell off. He was funny and reckless, but he was always there if you needed him.

Mimi, in many ways, was a second mom to me. For the first six years of my life, we slept in the same bed, and she was my defender if the boys teased me too much. She was the only person I ever let visit me in my little playhouse in Lancaster—and not because she was the only other person who could fit inside, but because I loved her so much. With four years separating us, Mimi was old enough to have her own set of friends and interests, so when I was a girl I spent a lot of time alone, but I was never lonely. I could spend an entire afternoon in the backyard singing the songs of the famous child singer Joselito from Spain or of my all-time favorite, Luis Mariano, and his greatest hit, "México." Sometimes I would sit for hours on my swing looking up at the sky, dreaming about all the wonderful possibilities life had to offer.

When I was not daydreaming, I was on the move. I loved sports, especially the ones involving speed. My very first pair of skates were hand-me-downs from my brother André; they were old, beaten-up and brown, without any picks on the blades to help me perform pirouettes and jumps. I fantasized about joining the Ice Capades and my parents scrimped to buy me a proper pair of white skates and pay for figure skating lessons. I loved the feeling of flying over the ice. I also enjoyed running and was fast enough to qualify for a regional race one summer. I was 12 and on the morning of the competition all the other competitors showed up with private coaches and wearing fancy adidas outfits. With my old running shoes and mismatched shorts and T-shirt, I suddenly felt like I did not belong. I lost my focus, lost the race and did not advance to the next level. It was the first time I had suffered from a severe lack of self-confidence, but it would not be the last.

When I was six years old, our family faced one of our biggest transitions when Dad had to move to Saratoga Springs, New York for a job. For the next 10 years, he could only come home for weekends. Because he was away and all the kids were in school full-time by then, Mom started working outside the home. She began as a waitress at banquets and loved being around people so much that, even after an eight-hour shift on her feet, she would float into the house with a big smile on her face.

Mimi—my fill-in, 10-year-old mommy—watched over me while Mom worked. We would go to the supermarket armed with a grocery list and money that Mom had left us. Mimi rolled me down the aisles in a shopping cart while I picked the items we needed from the shelf. She would calculate how much we were spending down to the penny to ensure we did not exceed our budget. We did household chores on Saturdays, and on the nights when Mimi cooked dinner, I would wash the dishes.

When Dad came home on weekends, he would bring a gift for Mom. He was always buying little presents to surprise her with—he would hide a pair of earrings in the cutlery drawer, leave a new dress laid out on the bed for her to find or tuck a love note into her mittens. In the evenings, Mom would sit on his lap on the narrow rocking chair in the living room and they would hold hands all night. I admired their tenderness and commitment; no matter how long or how often they were separated, they always found each other again. Mom was right: we were rich in love.

One of my favorite things about our Valleyfield house was how close it was to my school. Like Mom, I loved going to school and was so excited on my first day that I ran all the way, tripping and falling into a puddle before I got there. The teacher made me remove my wet tights and hang them on the radiator to dry in front of the entire class. There I was, standing in front of everyone in my gray tunic without any socks—what an embarrassing way to begin my formal education. But that did not stop me from making new friends and enjoying every one of my classes.

Also, like my mother, I was left-handed and encouraged by my teachers to write using my right hand—but at least I was not beaten across the fingers with a ruler as she had been. The only difficulty I had with a teacher during primary school was on the day we were asked to raise our hands and tell the class what we wanted to be when we grew up. Most of the kids gave the usual answer: fireman, nurse, pilot or doctor.

"I want to be a good person," I told the class.

"But that's not an occupation!" said the teacher, annoyed. "What do you want to *be*?"

I thought about it some more, but nothing else came to mind. All I wanted to be was a good person. I had been inspired by my parents' example—they were the best people I knew.

CHAPTER 3

Into the Dark

*J*UST BEFORE MY 14TH birthday, something happened that changed my life.

I was an independent-minded, determined adolescent and, one morning, I decided to totally change the way I looked. Without saying a word to anyone, I marched down to the hair salon, climbed into a chair and pointed to a picture of a fashion model sporting an extremely short, Mia Farrow-style hairdo.

"Can you give me the same cut?" I asked the hairstylist.

"Sure, no problem!" she said, and started cutting. Much to her surprise, and my horror, my hair—which had changed to a chestnut-brown shade from the original red I was born with—became kinkier and curlier with every snip. My eyes swelled and hot tears streamed down my cheeks; the more she cut, the more I cried. By the time she was finished, it was so curly that I looked more like singer Robert Charlebois or one of the Jackson 5 than the sleek-capped Mia Farrow. The stylist panicked and attempted to get the frizz under control by smearing giant gobs of Dippity-do into my hair. It made things worse—she ended up dumping an entire jar of the gloppy green gel onto my head and plastering it in. I slid from her chair and ran out the door sobbing, looking and feeling completely ridiculous.

While I was walking home, I saw my dad's Buick coming along the road and stopped to wait. I was embarrassed for him to see me, but I did not want to be on the street looking like that, either. Dad did not recognize me and drove past without slowing down. I walked all the way through town to our house, locked myself in my room and cried.

Something had broken inside of me—I was not the same. I am not being melodramatic, it was not just a bad haircut, it was a traumatic blow to my self-confidence—I felt utterly ugly and lost all self-esteem. Every time I looked in the mirror, my ruined hair reminded me of that loss.

"Guylaine, you may think you're an ugly duckling, but you are *beautiful*," my mom said, wrapping me in her arms. I did not believe her, but I loved her for saying it.

It took forever for my hair to grow out, and when it did, it was curlier and frizzier than ever. Back then, in the early 70s, long, straight hair was in style, and girls at school carried big combs in the pocket of their jean jackets. I carried one too, but it would have been pointless to use it on my Afro. Mom attempted to straighten the kinks with her steam iron, but it did not work. Dad tried to tease me out of my funk by holding a frying pan under my face, saying, "Laurette, looks like we're going to have sourpuss on the menu again tonight!" He made me so mad, but he was right. I had transformed from a happy young girl into a moody young woman and my moodiness would only get worse.

At 15, another painful incident wounded my fragile ego and left a deep and lasting impression. Mom bought me a brown, imitation leather winter coat that had fake fur covering the sleeves and a matching, bell-shaped hat. The ensemble looked very cool, and I felt proud and stylish wearing it to school for the first time. It was the one occasion I felt even a little bit pretty since my haircut fiasco a year earlier—a feeling obliterated after class when the school "mean girl" pelted me and my beautiful new coat with a dozen eggs. I was humiliated again, this time in front of my schoolmates. I walked home crying, certain my lovely outfit was ruined. Thank goodness for my resourceful mom, who wiped away my tears and the egg from my face and scrubbed the coat until it looked as good as new.

The girl who had attacked me never harassed me again—she was a bully to everyone and I guess that day it had been my turn to be her victim. Her cruelty was incomprehensible to me, but looking back on it, I hold myself partly to blame—my depression and self-pity had made me an easy target, attracting her anger like a magnet. But, at the time, that insight was still many years away.

Getting egged did not boost my popularity, and I was already the least popular student in the school. As a teenager, I was never part of the "in" crowd and never had a boyfriend. There were a few friends who tried to cheer me up and encourage me, but I was so down on myself that I was deaf to any positive suggestions.

My dark mood reflected back to me at home, where a painful family drama was unfolding.

One morning, instead of leaving for his job at the local garage, my brother Marcel sat down on a kitchen chair and started to cry. He cried nonstop, day and night, for a week and would not tell anyone what was wrong; he would not talk at all. He just sat in his chair and sobbed. It was a shock to all of us, especially because he had always been such an easygoing, happy guy with a lot going for him. He was in his early 20s, good looking, generous and sweet-natured—everybody liked him and he had friends all over town.

My poor parents did not know what to do. Mom worried he was using drugs; she searched the entire house, but found nothing. She called his friends and coworkers to see if they knew anything, but they were as confused by his behavior as we were. My other brothers pleaded with him to open up to them.

"Did somebody beat you up, Marcel? Did a girl hurt you? Do you owe money? Is someone threatening you?"

But he would not answer them—he just shook his head and cried. We could not understand what was wrong with him and he could not tell us, because he did not know either. Then one day he stopped crying as suddenly as he had started, but he still would not speak—not for weeks. The light went out of his eyes and he would look at us with the blank gaze of a zombie.

After a series of medical tests, Marcel was diagnosed with a bipolar disorder that was assumed to have been brought on by some sort of shock or emotional trauma. The doctors prescribed medication—but he was never the same, and we never found out what triggered his condition.

By then, my older brothers Réjean and Gaston were married and had their own homes and families, André had moved into an apartment across town and Mimi spent most of her time with her fiancé, Normand. So I was often alone at home with Marcel and my parents—thankfully, by then, Dad was back and working in Valleyfield.

The evenings were the worst. One night Marcel shuffled into my room wrapped in blankets and stood over my bed like a phantom in the dark. I awoke with a start.

"Guylaine," he murmured, staring at me from the shadows. "One day you'll find me dead in the basement; I want to kill myself to be done with this suffering." Then he turned and walked out into the hallway. I was so terrified he would attempt suicide that I stayed awake all night keeping watch, as I would for many nights to come. Whenever he went down into the basement, I felt my stomach clench.

On another occasion, he decided to make himself French fries in the middle of the night. He poured a bottle of cooking oil in a pot, put it on the stove with the heat on high and wandered off to bed. My parents and I woke up coughing on the thick black smoke filling the house.

It broke my parents' hearts, but it became impossible for them to care for Marcel. Despite his suicide threat, he was a gentle soul and never violent—but he refused to take his medication and that made him a danger to himself and the rest of us. A doctor eventually recommended Marcel be forced to leave home and live somewhere else.

"If he is on his own, he won't have his family to depend on and will be more likely to comply with his treatment," the doctor assured my parents. "It would be the best thing for him."

They were harsh words that went against everything my family believed in—taking care of others and of our own. But he was a doctor, and we did not know what else to do—there was such little awareness about mental illness back then. So, one summer night, the entire family gathered at the house to support Mom and Dad, who had reluctantly conceded to the doctor's advice. Mom packed Marcel a small suitcase and the boys walked him outside. Then we locked the door.

The horrible scene was burned into my memory and I will never forget the events of that night: all of us sitting inside while Marcel stood on the porch howling through his tears, ringing the bell and banging on the door, begging us to let him back in. Mom was crying hysterically, her heart shattering. Finally, she could not bear it anymore and began screaming as loudly as Marcel.

"Let him in! Let my boy in!" My brothers struggled to hold her back and prevent her from opening the door. "*Please!* Let him back in! We don't leave dogs outside, why should I leave my son?"

I don't know what was more agonizing—listening to Marcel pleading and pounding on the other side of the door, or seeing my mother trapped inside in such agony. Dad was so devastated he could not utter a word; he sat alone in a corner quietly weeping.

It was the "tough love" approach and the most painful experience my family had endured to that point. But after that terrible evening, Marcel agreed to take his medication. We rented him a small apartment close to home and he seemed happier there.

It was my fifth and final year of high school and I was carrying the anxiety of my home life to class with me and bringing my unhappiness at school back home, but I tried to keep my sadness to myself because my parents had enough to handle with Marcel. Even so, I was moody, withdrawn and so despondent it was hard to crawl out of bed in the morning. I hated myself and I resented Marcel for making me feel so miserable.

There was no reprieve from my weariness until I made a remarkable discovery one night as I lay in bed worrying about Marcel. If I closed my eyes and concentrated intensely on the black spot I envisioned on the inside of my forehead, I could feel myself melt into the Universe, where I would experience an amazing sense of calmness and peace. I was still conscious, aware that I had not fallen asleep, but I was somehow able to slip out of myself and away from my anxious mind. I began practicing the technique every night and soon I was having what some call out-of-body experiences.

Usually I would drift up toward my bedroom ceiling; sometimes I would float outside and evaporate into the dark. Once, I found myself in the house of a friend from school. I hovered over her while she and another friend watched TV and shared a bowl of popcorn. The next day I approached the girls at school and asked what they had been doing the night before.

"Just hanging out, watching TV and eating popcorn," they said. I smiled and asked what they had been watching and wearing. They gave me a funny look but described the exact television show and clothing I had seen during my "visit."

Their answers confirmed that my out-of-body experiences were real. I did not understand what they meant, but they convinced me that a great force existed beyond our comprehension, a force bigger than any of us. Years later I would discover that there are different planes of existence, but back then I knew nothing about other dimensions or astral travel. It was a huge mystery to me and I wanted to solve it—I wanted to know what was happening to me when I went "into the dark." But I had no one I could talk to about such a bizarre subject. I knew if I described my strange experiences to my family, friends or teachers, they would think I was crazy. And if I told a priest what I was doing at night, he may have suggested an exorcism or something! Besides, I had stopped going to church a year or two earlier. I was raised Catholic and my parents had taken us to Mass every Sunday as children, but by my teens, the dogma and rules no longer made sense to me or touched me spiritually. I believed God existed, but that He existed within each of us individually, and I wanted to feel His presence. Sometimes I would search for Him in the night sky; I looked up at the star that shone the brightest and somehow know I was being watched over and well-protected. Today, with my knowledge of palmistry and astrology, I realize I was looking at Jupiter, the planet of the Guru, or protector—the one who removes darkness. But back then I knew nothing of that.

So I kept my out-of-body experiences to myself, and at night I escaped from my troubles, at least temporarily, using my secret weapon that brought me such welcome peace.

One Sunday morning in July, not long after I had graduated from high school, I woke up early and looked at the clock: it was 6 a.m.

Oh, good, I thought. *I don't have to face the day yet; I can go back to sleep.*

Then, without effort and while fully conscious, I pulled out of my body and began gliding across the ceiling of my room while looking down at the sleeping Guylaine—and I did not like what I saw. I rushed down until I was on top of her, began beating her with my fists and shook her with all my might.

I sat up in terror. My heart was pounding: I had never been so frightened in my life. The experience shocked me to the core of my being, and I knew I had just sent myself a message: *Stop being miserable and feeling sorry for yourself.* I had to change, to shake myself free of my moodiness and stop blaming poor Marcel for my misfortunes and weariness, for my lack of success in life, for not having a boyfriend and being so unhappy. Instead, I had to love him with all my heart and help him as much as possible. In a flash of insight, I grasped just how selfish I had been and how drastically I needed to change my state of mind.

It was quite a wake-up call—I had to take responsibility for my own sorrows and my own happiness: I had no one to blame for my circumstances but myself.

In a matter of minutes my perception of Marcel completely changed, and so did our relationship. I really wanted to help him, and I learned to love him just as he was—my sweet brother. I will never forget that morning. My life took on a deeper dimension and a new direction.

CHAPTER 4

Higher Education

*A*FTER GRADUATING FROM HIGH school at 17, I was expected to know what to do with my life.

But how could I? The last five years had been filled with doubts and fears. How could I look to the future when I was haunted by my past? The one thing I was sure about was that I had to get out of Valleyfield and leave behind the feelings of failure that followed me everywhere.

I wanted to continue with my studies and had to decide on a program to enroll in at a CEGEP. (In Quebec, CEGEPs offer three-year professional programs or two-year pre-university programs.) When I tried to picture a career that would suit me, all I could come up with was acting. During high school, I had performed in a couple of school productions, including a musical, hoping it would take my mind off my difficulties, and it had helped. I thought I was a pretty good actor and singer, and, who knew, maybe I was destined for stardom.

I applied to audition for the theater program at Cégep Sainte-Thérèse. It was 80 kilometers away, which meant I could live on campus and still easily visit Valleyfield. It would be a fresh start in a new town where I could make new friends, I hoped. But when I arrived on campus for my audition, I wanted to turn around and go home. I had been pretty sheltered growing up and maybe I was too innocent and proper for this theatrical crowd, because I was shocked by what I saw. Most of the students looked like longhaired hippies, wearing ripped-up jeans and crazy dresses. Some were making out in public and others were smoking joints and drinking beer in plain sight.

What the heck will I learn in this kind of school? I wondered.

For my audition, I planned to perform a monologue about a girl who was lost in the woods, so I decided to do it barefoot. When it was my turn, I slipped off my shoes and took a deep breath, I was nervous because I had not prepared enough, but I was trying not to show it. The minute I stepped onto the stage, I lost all concentration—the floor was covered in so much filth and grime I could feel it oozing between my toes.

Oh, no! This is just not right, I thought, staring at the floor until someone at the back of the auditorium cleared his throat.

"Guylaine Vallée! Let's go! It's your turn. You're up!"

I froze.

"We're waiting. We don't have all day."

I could not open my mouth.

"Last time, Ms. Vallée … what do you have to show us?"

I just stared into the dark.

"Okay, get out!"

So I left. And I knew that was it, I would never set foot in that school again. I went back to Valleyfield—my first attempt to escape ended in failure and humiliation. And I did not have a backup plan. It was so late in the year that most schools were already at full enrollment and not taking any more applications. I was ready to give up on higher education when a friend told about an opening in the television program at Cégep de Jonquière's School of Media Arts and Technology. The program is quite famous today and boasts many well-known graduates and a long waiting list of students, but in 1977 it was pretty much unknown and, lucky for me, easy to get into. And the town of Jonquière was in the middle of nowhere, surrounded by forest and 500 kilometers north of Valleyfield—it would be my great escape. I applied shortly before the school year began and, thank goodness, I was accepted.

Mom and Dad were proud of me—Dad had been forced to quit school as a kid and Mom had dreamed of going to university. They had not had the money to send my older siblings to college, but they were better off now and offered to support me financially for the entire three-year program.

I lived in residence during my first year at Jonquière, and then moved into an apartment with some schoolmates for the final two years. It was a great experience. I was becoming independent, sticking to a budget, learning to be responsible and making friends. I was finally off to a fresh start.

I loved CEGEP life and was passionate about all of my classes—photography, publicity, marketing, television, scriptwriting, video editing and political science, to name a few. As I read more and more books and debated new ideas, I could feel my mind opening up and my awareness about the world expanding.

My first research assignment was on the Arab–Israeli conflict. I focused on Carlos the Jackal—the most infamous and most wanted terrorist of the time. Instead of writing a paper, I decided to perform a skit featuring myself in the starring role of The Jackal. My goal was for my classmates to experience the same type of terror Carlos was causing in so many countries. To create a sense of tension, I brought a plastic rifle with me and waited in the hallway for five minutes after the class had started. Then I knocked on the door and prepared to make a big entrance and play out the scene. The professor, however, was not impressed. He opened the door and gave me a look of disgust.

"What is this nonsense? You are late, Ms. Vallée. This is a classroom, not a theater! Get out!" I was humiliated once again, but now I was learning to go with the flow of life and I accepted my defeat without bitterness. It was a good thing I had maintained a fairly high average because, as well as losing my dignity in front of my classmates, I earned a big, fat zero on the assignment.

Even though my two recent attempts at theatrics—my botched performance as Carlos and my disastrous audition at Sainte-Thérèse—had bombed, I still believed I might have a future as an actor. I joined a theater group that was performing Michel Garneau's romantic comedy *Sur le matelas* (On the Mattress), about a young, honeymooning couple whose romance is constantly interrupted by various characters and circumstances. Our director, Dominique Lévesque, who became a well-known actor, did a great job—the play was a hit and we toured regional theaters in Saguenay and the region of Saguenay–Lac-Saint-Jean. I landed the starring role as the young bride and was paired with a good-looking actor who played my husband. But whenever I had to kiss him, I turned my head away from the audience, scrunched up my face and thought, *Ugh! Oh mon Dieu! I just can't!* There was zero chemistry between us—zilch! And I could not fake being romantic or pretend to feel something I did not, which, I suddenly realized, pretty much ended my career as an actor.

C'est la vie! At least I'll never have to do another audition.

I still dreamed of being a famous singer, but my desire to be an actor ended once the play was over, as did my melancholy over not having a boyfriend. My mind was too stimulated by everything I was learning to waste time and energy moping over my lack of a relationship. I was meeting all sorts of interesting people from across the province, and every Friday night a bunch of us went to the Café Campus and danced to Quebec's hottest bands, such as Harmonium, Beau Dommage and Les Séguin—I was finally having some fun!

When I felt down, I used my secret weapon at night, concentrating on the black spot at the center of my forehead to pull myself out of my body, allowing the peace of the Universe to wash over me. I used the technique less frequently as my depression subsided, but my out-of-body experiences still mystified me and made me want to explore my spirituality. My curiosity led me to a like-minded journalism professor with whom I became good friends and whom I trusted enough to confide in about traveling away from my body. I told him that those experiences proved to me we are all connected to a cosmic, universal force—a force I longed to connect with and understand.

He encouraged me to continue on my spiritual journey and we spent many hours discussing God, the soul and the purpose of existence. He was a member of the Rosicrucian Order, a metaphysical society that intrigued me so much that I wrote to their headquarters and applied for their lessons. Apparently they did not receive my application because I never heard back from them, which I took as a sign that my quest would lead me in a different direction.

My self-confidence was returning and I was now anxious to test myself, expand my horizons and explore the world. When I completed my three-year program, I won an internship at Radio Nord in Abitibi, Quebec, which was even further north and more remote than Jonquière. I worked as a sound technician for a television series called *Reflets d'un pays* (Reflections of a Country). We traveled a vast area of northern Quebec by small plane searching for human interest stories. It was a unique experience and I got to report on fascinating stories and people, such as the problems faced by teens on an Algonquin Indian reservation and the first couple in Quebec to move off the grid and build a solar-powered home in the bush.

It was rewarding work, which I did well enough to be offered a full-time position in Abitibi, but I felt removed from the larger world and wanted to live somewhere I could meet others who were searching for meaning and purpose, where I could make my mark and make a difference. When I woke up one morning in mid-June and saw snow falling outside my window, I knew Abitibi was not for me and that I really wanted to live in Montreal, my dream city!

But I had a problem, Montreal was a major media market— the big leagues—and I was barely out of school. I made phone calls and sent résumés to every TV studio and production company in town, but I did not receive a single callback.

Then I came up with a bold plan: I would go to Montreal in person and introduce myself as a producer who was preparing to shoot a television show and that I was in need of a director to review my script. At least that would get me in the door. *What the heck did I have to lose?*

I booked appointments with several directors and when I showed up, I handed them my résumé instead of a script. Usually I was ushered out the door, but eventually my boldness—or my desperation—paid off. One of the directors I had tricked burst out laughing and said, "Okay, I like your gusto, kid. I'll hire you."

And that was that—I was in Montreal! I rented a cute apartment in the Gay Village and was exhilarated by the neighborhood's energy and offbeat charm. Even though I had been hired on a short-term contract, I was certain I would soon be working full-time producing important documentaries and even writing and directing my own scripts one day. My prospects were bright and my future felt promising—until I showed up for work. It was a dismal experience, the job was monotonous and the people uninspiring—the highlight of my day was fetching coffee for executives who only cared about making as much money as possible and where they would go for lunch. It was passionless and no one was interested in sharing ideas or discussing spirituality or what was happening in the world. I found the same atmosphere surrounding me outside of work—the city and the people I met seemed shallow and materialistic. I could not make a meaningful connection with anyone and it was not long before I felt the familiar sense of emptiness and disillusionment growing inside me—the feeling that I did not belong here or anywhere.

I was rootless and alone and would spend the next year and a half feeling lost in Montreal, the "dream city" where I had hoped to find myself.

I only felt certain about one thing: I had not yet found what I was looking for.

CHAPTER 5

Paris, City of Lights and Hope

AFTER SPENDING A YEAR and a half in Montreal, moving from one meaningless job to the next, I had had enough. I knew I needed to make a major change, and make it quickly.

An opportunity presented itself when my friend Micheline and her boyfriend Lionel, who were sharing an apartment with me, suggested the three of us go backpacking in Europe for the summer.

"I know lots of people in Belgium, Norway and Sweden we can stay with," Lionel added. "We can find odd jobs to pay for our expenses. It'll be fun!"

While having fun sounded good, it was not all I was looking for. I was desperate to add purpose and meaning to my life and, who knew, perhaps that "purpose" was waiting for me in Europe. I told Micheline and Lionel to count me in. They did not know I was not planning a simple summer getaway; I was setting out on a spiritual quest, and it would take much longer than three months. I would need to stay in Europe for at least a year and, if I found what I was searching for, maybe forever. Micheline and Lionel purchased return tickets, but I sold all my furniture and appliances and bought a one-way ticket to Paris—much to my father's despair.

Dad could not understand why his 22-year-old daughter was giving up stability for an insane, backpacking trek across Europe. He had been so proud of me when I graduated from CEGEP and started forging a career, now he thought I was recklessly tossing it all away to live like a gypsy. It is one of the few times he was disappointed. He had never been good at expressing his emotions verbally and refused to talk to me on the phone as I prepared to leave.

Mom was worried too, but more sympathetic. She had a deep wisdom and knew without me having to tell her that I was looking for something I needed for my peace of mind.

"Be happy, beautiful girl," she said. "Do what you feel is right for you, but be happy."

Mimi, always the protective older sister, went to Dad to argue my case, but he foresaw only hardship and misery and was so upset he could not bring himself to come to the airport to see me off and say goodbye.

It pained me to hurt my dad; he had worked hard and sacrificed so much for his family during his life and, in return, he only hoped for their happiness. He was in my heart as I boarded the plane and on my mind during the entire seven-hour flight. I thought of how difficult it was for him to read and write because he had quit school to support his 10 siblings after his mother died. I remembered the little house he had built for me that had given me such happiness. And I recalled how he would try to cheer me from my misery as a teen with his silly pranks—like tying my big toe to my bedroom doorknob with a string if I refused to get out of bed and tugging it until I was forced to get up and face the day. He had never once let me down and I could not bear to think I had just done that to him.

When Mimi and her husband, Normand, dropped me off at the airport, they could see I was suffering. Normand hugged me and Mimi, God bless her, promised to make things right between Dad and me.

"Don't feel bad, Guylaine, go and have the best trip ever. We'll talk to Dad and make him understand. We promise."

By the time we landed in France, I felt better about how I had left things with my father and was excited to begin a journey that could reveal my destiny.

I fell in love with Paris the moment we touched down at Charles-de-Gaulle Airport; when I stepped off the plane I dropped to my knees and kissed the ground, just like the Pope does! I hoisted my brother André's enormous backpack onto my shoulder, boarded a bus with Lionel and Micheline, and headed into the City of Lights.

We stayed with Lionel's mother, a sweet, tiny woman who lived in the Maisons-Alfort, a modest suburb 9 kilometers from the center of town, and spent the next two weeks on a whirlwind tour of the city—walking the Avenue des Champs-Élysées, passing under the Arc de Triomphe, strolling along the Left Bank of the Seine, listening to street musicians and sitting in Notre-Dame Cathedral in awe of its timeless beauty.

No one in Paris could understand my Quebecois French accent and they laughed when I ordered a cup of coffee or bought a train ticket, but I did not care—I loved being there. The French culture washed over me and intoxicated me; just breathing the air energized me, and the food was more exquisite than I could ever have imagined. I can still savor the taste of the bread, cheese and pastries I sampled in the cafés that dotted every street.

We traveled by train from Paris to Belgium, where I felt oddly at home. Something about the windmills, cobblestone streets and lace curtains that hung in every window felt comforting and familiar. I had a similar sense of déjà vu crossing into Germany—but this time it was not at all comfortable. When we passed through customs and were questioned by armed officers, I broke into a cold sweat and my body shook. I had read a bit about reincarnation at CEGEP when I had investigated Rosicrucian beliefs—and I would learn much more about it when I discovered palmistry—but at the time, I did not connect past lives with the emotions I experienced in Belgium and Germany.

For three months after that, we traveled through Denmark, picked strawberries in Sweden and followed the Viking Trail through Norway, with its dazzling cliffs, glistening fjords and endless chains of snowcapped mountains. Compared to the flatness of my life in Montreal, my days felt full and three-dimensional—Valleyfield seemed a million miles away. It was a very romantic setting and Micheline and Lionel spent a lot of time alone, which made me reflect on love and not having a meaningful relationship of my own. The emptiness I had carried around since my teens was masked by the excitement and activity of the past few months, but I had not forgotten it, nor had I forgotten why I had come to Europe. When the summer ended, I returned to Paris to start building a new life.

I moved in with Lionel's mother. She was widowed and lived alone with her cat, so she welcomed my company. It was a run-down apartment building with few amenities in a humble, third-floor flat, not even a bathtub or shower, but it was affordable.

I took a seat at my regular table in the local café by 7 a.m. every morning and scoured the Want Ads over my morning espresso. It took weeks before I saw a job in my field, a posting by a video production and publicity company called Vidéo-France. They needed a host to work at the Cannes Film Festival.

What could be better than that? A job on the French Riviera, interviewing actors and directors about their latest films at one of the most prestigious awards ceremonies in the world!

I arranged an interview and arrived at Vidéo-France in my best outfit with résumé in hand. It was a modern, two-story building with a sweeping spiral staircase from the foyer to the executive suites on the upper floor. The office was buzzing with activity and it reminded me of an ant farm. Producers were rushing around with scripts and organizing camera crews to go out on shoots. It was the same hectic work atmosphere I had grown used to in Montreal. I felt right at home and I had a gut feeling the job was mine.

I was ushered up the winding staircase and introduced to the boss, who looked like a retired film star in his bright pink shirt and shocking white suit. He scanned my résumé and smiled, "You're Canadian? Good! We need someone who can speak English. You do speak English, right?"

My English was virtually nonexistent, a few words and phrases, but I crossed my fingers that it would be more than he knew.

"Yes, I can speak English."

"Okay, great! You're hired," he said. "But here's the thing—I'm not sending you to Cannes, because I need you to work here as a sound technician."

Before I could ask any questions, he took me for a tour of their massive, state-of-the-art recording studio. My stomach clenched when I saw the long rows of knobs, dials and levers. The only experience I had had as a sound technician had been holding a microphone.

"Are you familiar with this equipment, Guylaine?" he asked.

What could I say? I wanted to be in Paris and I needed the job.

"Sure I know how to use it!"

"Great! You start tomorrow."

The next morning I sat down in front of the recording desk completely clueless about how to make it work. I closed my eyes and put my finger on the biggest switch—hoping to turn on something without erasing anything. I was about to flip it when the boss walked in.

"Good morning, Guylaine. Ready to get started?"

Before I could answer, an assistant burst into the studio.

"We have an emergency! The video editor is sick and the project she's working on must be finished today!"

The boss turned to me, "Can you edit video?"

"You bet!" I answered, with total confidence. Video editing had been my specialty in school and I was an excellent editor. Ten minutes later, I was sitting behind the video console working like a pro. I was certain that God, or somebody "up there," was looking out for me.

My job was challenging and fun. I packaged highlight tapes of sporting events from across France that were sent to French embassies all over the world. I felt an extra sense of accomplishment whenever I saw my work being mailed to the ambassador in Quebec.

I also helped organize promotional video shoots, including one depicting a swanky soiree to promote Planters Peanuts, and my responsibility was to make sure the actors—and myself, as the company representative—were extremely well dressed. I was given an outrageous budget and I spent hours shopping for cocktail dresses in Paris's finest boutiques. I dressed in the latest trends and my first (and last) pair of high-heeled shoes. They were excruciating! I even dared to have my hair cut short again, this time in a professional European salon. The stylist gave me a very cool asymmetrical pixie cut, and this time I did not shed one tear.

My claim to be fluent in English came back to haunt me when there was a mechanical failure with the recording equipment. My boss arranged to fly in a technician from London the next day to repair it and would need me to translate for him. I ran out and bought an English–French pocket dictionary and stayed up all night trying unsuccessfully to teach myself a new language. The next day, I arrived at the office ready to confess my lie and admit I was not bilingual, but figured I would use up all the English I knew before handing in my resignation. When the technician walked in, I greeted him with one of the few phrases I knew: "How are you today?"

"*Ça va bien, merci!*" He spoke French! I sensed that somebody up there was watching over me and protecting me, just as I had years before looking up at the stars in the night sky searching for God.

I worked hard and put in long hours at the job, even volunteering to work Saturdays. Sundays were mine, reserved for exploring the city. I walked all over Paris and lived centuries of history. I lost myself for entire days among the ornate mausoleums in the Père Lachaise Cemetery, where creative geniuses were laid to rest—from Chopin, Molière, La Fontaine, Balzac and Proust to Seurat, Oscar Wilde and Édith Piaf. I was mesmerized by the masterpieces at the Louvre, toured Versailles and Marie-

Antoinette's castle, and looked up at Napoleon's towering tomb in the Museum of War.

Paris had so much to offer—so much culture and beauty to enjoy—and I wanted to share that enjoyment with someone. But I did not meet anyone I was interested in romantically and no one I met seemed interested in me. After my exciting Sunday outings, I would return to my dim, unwelcoming apartment and find Lionel's mother already asleep. She was kindhearted, always leaving me leftovers in the oven to warm up, and I spent many evenings in the City of Lights sitting at her drab kitchen table beneath a bare lightbulb eating alone.

While in Paris I became fascinated with World War II, and whenever I encountered someone who had lived in Paris at that time, I asked about their experiences. Their stories were as fresh as they were painful and, ever since my frightening experience at the German–Belgium border, I could not shake the feeling I had somehow shared in that trauma. It made me wonder how many lifetimes we spent passing through this world, and why? What was the purpose of suffering from one life to the next, enduring war, loss and heartache? Where did it lead us to in the end? And what was the end? I did not know then that the answers to those questions were in the palm of my hand.

Every few months, I had to make a weekend trip to Spain or Switzerland to have my passport stamped because Vidéo-France had agreed to hire me without a French work visa and I needed my visitor status renewed. I was making good money but I continued to stay with Lionel's mother to save cash. Her yellow cat would wait in the third-floor windowsill and watch for me on the street every evening when I returned from work, like she was making sure I got home safe.

One night, I did not feel so safe. I had left work after dark and when I stepped off the train near home, I was surrounded by three men who pushed me up against a wall and pulled out knives. I was about to have my throat slit when one of them called off the attack.

"Wait, she lives around here. We're not touching her," he said, and they walked away.

Yet again, I had the powerful feeling that I was being watched over and divinely protected. But the assault had shaken me and made me remember how alone I was. *What would my life have amounted to had I ended up dead on the dirty floor of a train station on the outskirts of Paris?*

On the surface, I seemed to have it all—I was young, with fancy clothes and a high-paying, exciting job in the most romantic city in the world. But I had set out on a quest for purpose and meaning and after more than a year in Paris, the familiar void was expanding at the center of my being. It had never left me; I had only succeeded in burying it beneath a bit of glamor.

So, when the boss called me into his office to say the company was bankrupt and closing down, I was glad to head back to Canada. I bought a plane ticket, packed up my new Parisian clothes, tucked the $2,000 I had saved into my shoe, and headed back to Charles-de-Gaulle.

After 15 months in Europe, I was on my way home with a wealth of experience and knowledge, but as lost as ever and still in search of my purpose in life and my true destiny.

CHAPTER 6

The Man in the Golden Slippers

WHEN I RETURNED TO Montreal, I landed a job as a TV scriptwriter and rented a loft in Saint-Louis Square, a bohemian neighborhood filled with artists and an ambiance that reminded me of Paris. My job paid well and kept me busy, but besides the occasional bit of excitement, my life was still empty and unfulfilling. I would go for long walks at night, look up toward Venus shining above and talk to God. *Help me find something to make sense of my life. I feel lost. I don't care about money or fame; I need a mission.*

There's a saying: When the student is ready, the teacher will appear. At the age of 24, I was finally ready. Six months after returning from Paris, some girlfriends from Valleyfield dropped by my loft for a visit. We were talking about jobs and careers, and one of the girls mentioned that her sister had worked for an East Indian palmist in Montreal named Ghanshyam Singh Birla.

Something clicked in me. I had never heard his name before, but I knew I had to meet him. It was not that I was fascinated by palmistry or that I believed someone could stare into a crystal ball and predict my future. I had gone to a palmist once when I was in school in Jonquière and just beginning my spiritual quest. The man took $30 from me (a fortune back then), sat me down in his "office" beside the kitchen sink in his apartment and glanced at my hands for a couple of minutes.

"You have nice legs—like a dancer; you will drop out of school and you are going to have twins."

I wanted to kill him. I loved school and would never have dropped out. And even as a young teen, I had babysat enough kids to know that I adored babies, but motherhood was not for me. And how unprofessional to check out my legs! The man was a total fraud and the experience completely turned me off palmistry.

So it was not his occupation, but the sound of Ghanshyam's name that resonated with me. My gut feeling was that this man could guide me to the path I needed to follow. I called his office the next day to set up an appointment, and was frustrated to find out that they could not fit me in for another month and a half. Apparently he was very popular—the earliest I could book a session was the afternoon of May 4. I agreed to the date, but I called almost every day while I waited, hoping there might be a cancellation (there was not). I knew nothing about astrology at the time, but in the not-too-distant future I would learn that, according to my astrological chart, May 4, 1984 was a particularly auspicious day for me to meet Ghanshyam—it was a day worth waiting for.

On the morning of my appointment, I woke up with more excitement and enthusiasm than I had felt in months. *Could this be the day I finally discover what I've been searching for?*

I wore my most colorful clothes from Paris, including my electric blue leather pants that went so well with my bleached, pixie haircut. My outfit's pièce de résistance was a transparent plastic purse with a huge plastic fish inside—a one-of-a-kind Paris original!

The Palmistry Center was across town in the Montreal neighborhood of Westmount and during the long ride on the Number 24 bus I thought of questions to ask the palmist, all of which I forgot the moment I arrived at 351 Victoria Avenue and saw the sign: *The Birla Center for Hast Jyotish.*

When I opened the door an alarm chimed with the sound of songbirds, whose sweet singing followed me up the stairs into the reception area, fragrant with the soothing aroma of burning incense. I felt as though I had just climbed up to heaven.

A woman with long, black hair named Lydia met me in the lobby and led me to a sink, where she used a little rubber paint roller to coat my hands with black ink. She then pressed each of my palms onto a sheet of blank, white paper. And there they were: my handprints. I had no way of knowing that I was looking at my two new best friends—friends that held the secrets of my past, the path to my future and the key to unlock them both. When I saw my prints for the first time, I was shocked at how crooked my fingers were and how big my hands looked. I felt a little exposed, knowing that my hands—and all they might reveal about me— would soon be scrutinized by the eyes of an expert.

This is it, the moment of truth.

I washed the ink from my hands and sat down to wait for my reading. A few minutes later, Ghanshyam walked into the room. I was struck by how dignified he looked in his beige Nehru suit—and a pair of golden slippers! I was amazed someone could be confident and comfortable to wear slippers to work. He had a thin, black moustache and penetrating brown eyes that lit up like birthday candles as he welcomed me with a warm smile.

Oh my! He looks even more beautiful than before, I thought, feeling a powerful surge of déjà vu. *Guylaine, don't be silly! This is the first time you've ever seen him!*

"Hello, hello, *helloooo*! It is *so* nice to meet you!" Ghanshyam said in a sweet, lilting East Indian accent. He took my hands in his and shook them with such genuine affection—it felt like a reunion with a long lost friend. He radiated with an honest-to-goodness kindness that put me instantly at ease.

"Please, come with me, my dear."

I followed him into his office, which was dominated by an armoire filled with books about palmistry and astrology, many of them worn by age and use, bearing titles in languages I did not recognize. A large portrait of an Indian man wearing an orange robe hung above Ghanshyam's desk. The man's face was serene and his eyes were half-shut in a trancelike state. His arms were raised with open palms, as though he were bestowing a blessing upon me while I took my seat.

A translator joined us for the session, as Ghanshyam spoke no French and the extent of my English was "How are you today?" She informed me that Ghanshyam practiced Vedic palmistry, a form of traditional Indian palmistry that originated in the ancient Hindu scriptures known as the Vedas.

Ghanshyam placed the paper with my handprints on the desk, next to my astrological chart, which he had drawn up before my arrival. I had been unaware that astrology was related to palmistry, but I learned they are twin sciences and that *hast jyotish* is a phrase combining two Sanskrit words—*hast*, meaning hand, and *jyotish*, meaning light. So *hast jyotish* described the light from our planets being reflected in our hands.

After studying my chart and making all sorts of notes and scribbles on my prints with various colored pens, Ghanshyam looked up at me. His brown eyes shone with such intensity I felt he was staring into my soul.

"Let's begin, shall we?" His voice had the tone of a compassionate doctor who had examined a patient's X-rays and had both good and bad news to deliver.

"You are on a mission to find God and you have been on this quest for a long time," he said, "but you haven't made a spiritual connection. You're miserable because you are stuck in one place and have no direction, which has made you feel lost and alone. You can't decide what to do, and that has left you without any meaning or purpose in your life. Does that sound right to you?"

I was too overwhelmed to speak. He knew exactly what I had been feeling for the past decade—as if he had known me my entire life. I nodded.

He looked down at my prints and began pointing to various lines with his pen.

"Look here. Your destiny line is fragmented, your Sun line is barely existent, your thumb lacks distance from your Jupiter finger, and just below that … your Mount of Jupiter is depleted and your Venus lacks balance."

I was lost in the details, not understanding a word of the technical aspects of palmistry. I did not know at the time that we all have a dominant hand (the one we write with) that reveals our present life, and a non-dominant hand that reveals our past life—let alone that how we hold our thumbs reveals our level of willpower and self-confidence. The flood of data was dizzying, but when Ghanshyam finished his initial analysis his conclusions were painfully accurate.

"You have 12 flaws that are blocking you—they are undermining your spiritual growth and making your destiny unclear. You feel uncomfortable in the world and have closed yourself off—and that is making you unhappy."

Then, in quick succession, he wrote down 10 of the flaws on my handprint sheet, in the space between the dark, inky images of my two palms.

– No decision
– No willpower
– No direction
– No discipline
– No motivation
– No inspiration
– No single mindedness
– No meditation
– No exercise
– No intellectual and/or spiritual work, which will give you hope, trust, joy, faith and a sense of identity

His pen hovered for a moment and then, at the top of the page, he added what he said were my greatest flaws of all: no faith in myself and no self-confidence.

"You have a good head line, great intelligence; I'm sure you will find success in your career. But," he said, shaking his head, "you will probably continue to feel the same sense of emptiness."

He tapped his pen against my print, in the center of my left palm.

"Your destiny line suggests you could find something that gives you happiness, but not until your early forties."

Oh my God, I have to live like this for another 20 years? I could not imagine the misery of such a long, unhappy life.

Tears were streaming down my face. Ghanshyam, who had been very calm and respectful through the reading, slid a box of tissues toward me.

"Don't be upset, the lines on our hands aren't carved in stone—this isn't fortune-telling. Our palms show us what we need to change in our life to find happiness. When we make those changes, the lines on our hands will change. Real palmistry is not about prediction, it is about prevention, about growth!" he said with that same smile he had greeted me with.

"But my question for you, Guylaine, is this: Do you want to change, or do you want to stay like you are?"

"*I want to change*, Ghanshyam," I sobbed.

"*Gooooood!* Then you *will* change!" he announced happily, throwing his arms open and letting out a booming, hearty laugh. "That makes all the difference!"

He fixed his gaze upon me again, disappearing into his own thoughts for a few moments. Then he returned to my sheet with his pen and wrote "12 MONTHS" above my handprints.

"You have a mission in life; you will be of service to many people. But your mission won't begin for another year, not until you're ready."

My heart was pounding so hard, all I could hear for a few seconds was a steady *thud, thud, thudding* in my ears. Then, all I heard was the echo of his words: *You will have a mission in life; you will be of service to many people.*

Ghanshyam's words were a balm on my aching soul.

He suggested steps I could take to "open myself up" and prepare for what life had in store for me. He explained that certain gems and metals correct imbalances in the body's energy system and promote spiritual growth. He gave me a list of precious stones to buy and suggested I read *Autobiography of a Yogi* by Paramahansa Yogananda. Ghanshyam pointed to the picture of the man in the orange robe above his desk, whom I now felt had been watching over me since I had entered the room.

"Paramahansa's book could help you a great deal," Ghanshyam said. Then he suggested we meet every other week for five more sessions.

"We will devise a program together that will help you to develop trust and confidence in yourself and make the changes you need to bring great joy into your heart and find peace of mind. And then you'll see, Guylaine—your life will fill up with friendship and trust and love! How about that!"

Ghanshyam had delved deep into my heart during our hour-long session, and when he walked around the desk to give me one of his enormous hugs that I would come to love, I wanted to jump into his golden slippers.

"Don't worry, everything will be fine," he promised.

This man I had never met before, who came from another continent and a different culture, had just touched my heart like no one else had ever done.

I was certain that my life was about to change. As I left his office I felt something I hadn't in a long time—I was happy.

CHAPTER 7

True Calling

*M*Y MEETING WITH GHANSHYAM convinced me I could change my life for the better and I wanted that change to begin immediately.

Before I left the Palmistry Center, I booked five more sessions, ordered the gems Ghanshyam prescribed and headed to the nearest bookstore to find a copy of Paramahansa Yogananda's *Autobiography of a Yogi*—the book he said would help me.

The store clerk said they only had the English version in stock—which, of course, I could not read—and offered to order a French version for me. But I was determined to get that book *today*. I checked the shelves myself and found one copy—it was in French! I did a victory dance to the counter.

"Well, whad'ya know!" the clerk laughed. "It must have been waiting for you. I've never seen anyone so excited to buy a book."

I started reading as soon I got home and was instantly addicted—*Autobiography of a Yogi* is about a spiritual quest! The beauty, sincerity, purity and humor of Paramahansa's words pulled me into a completely new world and did not let me go. He was born in India in the late 1800s, and from the moment of his birth he was searching for God and working to become a better person and fulfill his mission in life. I loved learning about Indian culture and Vedic philosophy, and the tale itself was such a wild and wonderful spiritual adventure that I had to remind myself it was a true story. And the truth Paramahansa shared spoke directly to my heart: God lives in each of us, and we can meet and talk to Him by raising our consciousness.

There was so much to learn in *Autobiography* that I knew I would reread it many times over the years, which I have. But my first reading was special—it introduced me to Kriya Yoga, a method of meditation to help speed one's journey to God. In the early 1920s, Paramahansa came to America and built the Self-Realization Fellowship (SRF) in Los Angeles to teach Kriya Yoga and share his wisdom with the Western world. *One day I am going to visit that place and I am going to learn Kriya Yoga.*

It took me two weeks to finish the book, just in time for my second session with Ghanshyam. He gave me another warm welcome and was happy I had read *Autobiography*; he was very much a devotee of both Paramahansa and Kriya Yoga.

In our early sessions, Ghanshyam went over some basics of palmistry with me. He explained that our three levels of consciousness—the conscious, subconscious and superconscious—are reflected in every part of our hand, from our fingers to the major and minor lines crisscrossing our palms to the fleshy pads of the palm known as "mounts."

It was lucky I had switched from being left-handed to right as a schoolgirl, he told me, because the head line on my left hand was shorter.

"Your right hand is your dominant hand, and it tells us about your life right now, but that's just the tip of the iceberg. Nine-tenths of what has shaped your personality is found in your left hand. Your left hand is a window into your subconscious and into your past (and past lives, I would later discover). The head line in your left hand reveals how you've perceived the world around you. Now look here," he said, taking my left hand and tracing his finger along the head line in the center of my left palm.

"See how short the head line on your left hand is? This tells us you've been so insecure and worried about what people think that you haven't been able to develop confidence in yourself. Unless we fix this line, you could subconsciously carry a big bag of insecurities around your neck for the rest of your life. We don't want that, do we?"

At Ghanshyam's recommendation, I started to wear a coral and garnet pendant to help build my confidence, conviction and self-assurance. He had studied gemology and even wrote a book on the subject. Gems and precious metals, he said, had been used for thousands of years in India to boost physical and spiritual health. Garnet and coral corresponded to Sun and Mars, two "hot planets" that would fire me up. I also began wearing a beautiful, nine-gem ring (representing all the planets) to make me more receptive to the positive energy around me.

As my sessions with Ghanshyam progressed, we delved more deeply into the world of palmistry. Sometimes it seemed a little esoteric and wild to me–like the day Ghanshyam tried to teach me about the body's electrical system and the seven chakras or "energy centers" located along the length of our spine.

"Imagine it like intertwining 'wires' coiled around your spinal column that carry electrical currents of male and female energy. We have to get that electrical energy flowing in you, Guylaine—we have to recharge you!"

I smiled and nodded, but I was thinking: *What's all this stuff about wiring? If I wanted a lesson in electricity, I'd call up Réjean and get it from my brother, the electrician! I'm paying for this?*

I am sure Ghanshyam picked up on my skepticism but, wonderful teacher that he is, he carried on good-naturedly knowing one day I would appreciate and understand the value of what he was offering me. Whenever I listened to the taped recordings of my sessions, I could hear just how unreceptive I sometimes was to his wealth of information.

And I was reminded that I had "12 flaws," which included a resistance to intellectual and spiritual work. I vowed to be more open. When he explained that our breath was the essence of our life force—what he called "prana"—and taught me to breathe along the spine to awaken my chakras, I actually felt myself opening up and that electric energy start to flow. It turned out Ghanshyam was a master electrician!

In another session, he pointed out my tendency to keep my thumbs tucked into the palm of my hand.

"Your thumb is an extension and expression of your Mount of Venus—the mount of love. When you hide your thumb, you cut yourself off from giving and receiving love and the powerful creative energy love possesses. It's like locking your vitality and joy in a dark basement and throwing away the key. You're trapped inside yourself, feeling ugly and unwanted. When you look outside and see other people in love and being happy, you feel weak and powerless and unlovable."

"It's true, Ghanshyam," I told him, sadly. "I don't feel good in my body; I want to love and feel loved, but I don't feel beautiful enough to attract those good things."

"Guylaine, this little thumb of yours is part of what's preventing you from being who you're meant to be—you live in a constant state of fear and stress and aren't even aware of it. You're fragile and vulnerable—but that's not who you are. With your strong Sun finger and mount and a Moon in Leo, you should feel alive and dynamic! That is the real you!"

Ghanshyam taught me several breathing exercises to open my chest and reduce tension, and encouraged me to write to the SRF headquarters to request "energization" exercises that had been developed by Paramahansa, which I did.

"These aren't ordinary exercises; they help direct cosmic energy to us, develop our concentration and center our breath. That prepares us to practice meditation—and meditation is the spiritual foundation of our lives. But you aren't ready to meditate yet—we must be patient."

He suggested I hang a sign over my bed that read "Let Go and Let God."

"When you wake up in the morning and go to bed at night, you'll be reminded not to worry about what you can't control and to focus on what's most important."

Developing focus came up in another session when he pointed out that my destiny line was underdeveloped.

"You have a rich subconscious, but aren't tapping into its creative potential and using it to express who you really are. You're like a leaf blown about by the wind," he said, lifting his hand and fluttering his fingers from left to right in front of me.

"You must dedicate yourself to one passion and pour yourself into it with your entire being—be single-minded! Otherwise you could spend your entire life searching for your destiny instead of living it."

He highlighted the importance of cultivating a single passion by sharing a story about the famous figure skater Toller Cranston. Early in his career, Toller consulted Ghanshyam because he was torn between his desire to skate and his passion for painting.

"I told him what I'm telling you, Guylaine—to be a success, he had to choose one passion and focus on it. And because he was young, he had better choose skating and not pick up a brush until he realized his dream of becoming a world champion skater. That's what he did, and that's what you must do—eliminate the dreams that distract you, find your true passion and pursue it with all your heart. You must find your true calling!"

When that session ended, Ghanshyam invited me to attend a class he was giving that evening on the head line. Even though he was teaching in English, I promised to be there. I was eager to learn everything I could about palmistry and figured something was bound to sink in.

I went to a restaurant across the street for dinner before the class and was glad to find it was empty; I wanted to eat in peace and reflect upon what Ghanshyam had said about opening up my thumb and finding my true calling. But it must have been a popular eatery, because by the time my meal arrived, the place was packed solid and noisy as a carnival. There was so much chatter, I could not hear myself think, but I had no trouble hearing a couple sitting at the opposite side of the restaurant. Their peals of laughter cut through the din and echoed in my ears. They were smiling and laughing so much I could not concentrate on my soup—and I could not take my eyes off them. They seemed so *happy!* All that happiness irritated me because it reminded me how I longed to feel the same way. I pulled my folded thumb out of my palm and paid my bill.

The reception area at the Center had been transformed into a classroom when I returned, and it was quickly filling with students. My lack of English had me feeling self-conscious and I found a seat in the very back row, incognito. But when the couple from the restaurant walked into the room I sat up and took notice.

It was the first in a series of lectures on the head line and when Ghanshyam introduced his staff members before the class began, I discovered that the "happy couple" were sister and brother—Kathy and Peter Keogh—and that they worked at the Palmistry Center.

Ah! That's why they are so happy! They work with Ghanshyam!

Kathy had been working with Ghanshyam for a decade and Peter had been with the Center for several years. Like Ghanshyam, they radiated a friendliness and warmth that was contagious, and I wished I had taken a front row seat to be closer to them.

Ghanshyam's head line class was amazing. I did not understand a word he said, but that did not matter—I was starting to grasp that palmistry is the language of the soul, which Ghanshyam spoke with such fluency and passion I did not need a translator to understand his message: palmistry can change our lives. He demonstrated this fact by showing before-and-after handprints of clients he had helped over the years. The evidence was there in front of me: even without any technical knowledge of palmistry, I could see the lines in the before-pictures were blocked and broken, whereas in the after-pictures they were solid and clear.

After the class, Ghanshyam introduced me to Kathy and Peter, and we clicked immediately. Kathy gave me a big hug before I left and my gut feeling told me we were going to be great friends.

When I got home that night I looked down at my palms and wondered how long it would be before my own lines changed, and what my life would be like once they had.

Around that time, both my contract as a TV scriptwriter and my sessions with Ghanshyam came to an end. I decided to volunteer at the Center because they helped people and I wanted to be a part of the good they were doing. It also felt like a second home to me by then and I thought it would be the perfect place to follow Ghanshyam's advice and figure out what my true calling was.

One Saturday afternoon, I was in the office with Peter and we had a long heart-to-heart chat. He was an excellent listener and, I discovered, a talented musician and passionate student of human behavior. He was very good at helping people with their problems and had planned to become a psychologist—in university he had studied both psychology and music, but he changed career paths after meeting Ghanshyam and eventually devoted himself to the Center full-time.

"Ghanshyam made me aware of a new method of understanding human behavior that was an effective way to help people *and* deeply spiritual," he said.

He had found his true calling, but how was he able to abandon his passion for music and psychology and focus only on palmistry? He did not abandon them, he told me—he combined his love of music and interest in human behavior and poured them both into palmistry. Peter produced beautiful meditation mantras with his music and used his knowledge of psychology while reading palms—palmistry, after all, was a form of universal psychology.

As it turned out, being at the Center was exactly what I needed to narrow my focus and eliminate two secret ambitions of my own that had long been a source of distraction and frustration.

The first ambition was disposed of during a recording session with Peter, Ghanshyam and musician Serge Fiori. I had not told anyone at the Center about my dream of one day becoming a famous singer or that Serge Fiori was a musical hero of mine.

(Certainly no one knew I sang along to his songs in the shower!) But Ghanshyam has a way of sensing a person's hidden desires and he invited me to sing with Serge during their recording of a meditation mantra. I jumped at the opportunity, but I became so shy and self-conscious when it was my turn to perform that I mumbled incoherently instead of singing. It was an even worse performance than my acting school audition—a total disaster! My dream of singing stardom evaporated, which was a blessing—one less distraction cluttering up my destiny list.

My second buried ambition was to become a writer. I had written plenty of informational TV scripts, but I had always dreamed of producing a truly great drama. And as it happened, the Canadian Broadcasting Corporation was sponsoring a writing contest—the winner would receive $5,000 and would have their script produced. But it would require a full-time commitment of several months and I was torn between writing and volunteering at the Center. Ghanshyam had helped me so much and I wanted to return his kindness—but he had also taught me that I could not pursue several dreams simultaneously and expect to find success or happiness.

Ghanshyam made the decision easy for me. It was a sunny, summer afternoon and Peter and I were painting the roof of the Center when Ghanshyam came up to say hello. He was on crutches after seriously injuring his foot a few days earlier and I rushed over to him to help him with his briefcase. As soon as our eyes met, I blurted out my dilemma in broken English.

"Guylaine the writer! That's wonderful!" he said, with his beautiful smile. "Go and write the best script ever. And remember—if you win, I win with you!"

I was deeply touched and I promised myself that if I won the contest, I would donate half the prize money to the Center.

So I left in search of my destiny. For the next six months, I immersed myself in writing *Faux pas*, a dark, complicated drama about a depressed teen who is battling issues of abuse and her inability to fit into society. It was one of the most painful periods of my life. The loneliness and isolation of being a writer were suffocating and I ached for my friends at the Center. I guess my writing reflected my depression: my script placed 94th in the contest. I was crushed.

It was Christmastime but I was feeling no joy. I was overwhelmed with a sense of failure and shame—the only person I wanted to see or talk to was the man in the golden slippers. I called the Center and booked an appointment with Ghanshyam for early January.

When I opened the door of the Center a few weeks later, the familiar sound of happy birds welcomed me home. Ghanshyam threw his arms open and asked in his hearty, booming voice:

"*Soooo*, did you write a great script? Did you win?"

"No, I didn't." I burst into tears.

"Come with me," he said gently, giving me a hug. "Let's see what's going on with you."

In his office, Ghanshyam looked at my palm and told me not to worry.

"So the script didn't work out—dry your tears. All you need is a couple more sessions with me and everything will be fine!" I started to laugh, and so did he. He reminded me that when I first came to him, I was desperately searching for happiness and meaning.

"But you weren't looking in the right place, Guylaine. The only place you can find peace or joy is within yourself. And you weren't equipped for an inner journey back then—you had to satisfy all your desires before you were ready for soul searching. Now you are ready! So, you see—you did win!"

Ghanshyam invited me to join him and the rest of the staff that evening for a special meditation commemorating the birth of Paramahansa Yogananda. I went to buy flowers and prayed hard that Ghanshyam was right, that I was now ready to look within myself without fear or doubt. As I walked through the snow, it occurred to me it had been almost a year since I had called the Center and booked my first session. Suddenly, I remembered what Ghanshyam had told me during that reading—I had a mission in life, but a year would pass before I was ready to take it on.

How could I have forgotten such an important message!

Now that I remembered, I instinctively knew what my mission was: to become a better person and dedicate my life to helping others do the same. And I knew where my mission would begin.

At our next session I told Ghanshyam I was ready to join the Center; I wanted to learn palmistry and work with him.

"Good!" Ghanshyam said, with a loud clap of his hands. "We'll check the chart and choose a good day for you to start, a day with a good Moon to ensure you have the greatest possible success."

The best day was Monday, March 18, 1985—my official start date at the Palmistry Center.

A few days later, the gang took me to a Chinese restaurant to celebrate my 25th birthday. My mind was at peace and my heart was full of joy. At one point during the evening, I looked over at Ghanshyam and saw rays of red and golden light emanating from him—he was surrounded in a brilliant, shimmering halo. I blinked my eyes to clear them, but the incredible light was still there, glowing even more intensely.

I had never seen anything like it—it was breathtaking and beautiful. There was obviously something very special about this man; at that moment, I knew he would be my teacher and mentor. I would surrender to his wisdom and trust him to guide me on my journey to become a better person.

My primary school teacher had told me that being a good person was not an occupation, but she was mistaken—I had found my true calling.

CHAPTER 8

Finding My Center

NOT EVERYONE WAS AS happy as I about my decision to become a palmist.

Some friends were certain I had been lured into a cult; others whispered about drug use or thought I was having a nervous breakdown. My roommates were openly hostile toward palmistry, mocking me when I studied my handprints at home or curled up on the couch to read *Autobiography of a Yogi*.

No matter what I said to defend my change in lifestyle and career, I was met with rolled eyeballs and sneers. My ego was still fragile and I could feel their negativity and disdain eating away at the foundation of my new life. Drastic measures were needed if I hoped to keep my dream alive, so I cut off all ties with my old friends and moved into a tiny apartment in a new neighborhood within walking distance of the Palmistry Center.

My family was worried too, but they were easier to persuade that my choice would not lead to ruin. Dad had predicted disaster when I had moved to Europe a few years earlier with only a couple of dollars in my pocket and a quest in my heart. But I ended up getting a high-paying job in Paris and managing just fine, so I guess he figured I would be okay at the Palmistry Center, even if he had no clue what a palmist did. Mimi always supported me no matter what, and the boys had long considered me a free spirit and were not surprised when they heard the news. My supportive mother said what she always said, "As long as you're happy, I'm happy."

Nevertheless, my parents could not help being anxious about me entering such an obscure and eccentric profession, and I could not blame them. Palmistry had been banned in Montreal just a few years earlier under archaic, anti-witchcraft laws and one foreign-born astro-palmist was actually deported from the country. Fortunately, no one in the family thought of me as a witch, and the silly law was largely ignored and eventually removed from the books.

Just before I started work at the Center, my old boss, Claire, a television producer, phoned me with a job offer.

"Guylaine, I have great news for you. I've booked you as the scriptwriter for a new 13-episode series, and it pays even more than before."

It was a high-profile job with a lot of money.

The Palmistry Center could not pay me much—shockingly little, in fact. I was not even sure if I would be able to cover the rent on my new apartment once my savings were spent. It dawned on me that I had committed to palmistry without checking to see if I could actually earn a living at it. I knew this scriptwriting job would build up my bank account and cement my future in the television industry. But it was not the future I wanted.

"Claire, I've just accepted a new job," I said.

"Oh? At which production company?"

"It's not a television job. I'm going to work at the Palmistry Center."

"At the what?"

"The Palmistry Center, in Westmount."

"What do you mean? What are you doing *there*?"

I knew exactly what I would be doing at first.

"Sorting mail and making tea, to start."

"Why in God's name would you want to do that? I'm offering you 13 weeks as a scriptwriter at top dollar, and I can offer you an expense account."

"But what happens after 13 weeks?"

"You should be happy with 13 weeks!"

"What about the rest of my life?"

"You're crazy, Guylaine," she said, and hung up.

With that, I cut the last tie to my old life.

A few days later, on the auspicious Monday morning that had been chosen as my start date, I arrived at the Center to begin my new career. There was a big bouquet of flowers waiting on my desk with a note from Ghanshyam: "Welcome to the Palmistry Center, Guylaine! We are blessed and fortunate to have you with us." It was sweet, but I knew it was I who had been blessed.

The Center had a small staff—just seven people, including me—and a long waiting list of clients. No wonder it had taken me nearly two months to get my first appointment! Back then, Ghanshyam and Kathy did all the readings and consultations. When they weren't in the office for sessions with clients, they were preparing teaching material for their classes, developing a new training program for palmists and organizing the Center's ever-growing database of handprints. By the early 80s, they had already amassed thousands of prints: one of the largest collections of handprints in the world. Sometimes they were so busy they did not stop to eat, and so I prepared lunch for them and did what I could to make their lives as pleasant as possible. The Center opened at 9 a.m. sharp six days a week and Ghanshyam would finish his final consultations of the day at 9:00 p.m. After that, clients who lived in different time zones would begin calling in for phone consultations. I would not leave the office until Ghanshyam did, and it was not unusual for me to answer the phone well after midnight to hear the distressed voice of someone in the midst of a personal crisis, insisting it was a matter of life or death that they speak to Ghanshyam *immediately*. Ghanshyam never refused a call, and on those occasions he often did not leave for home until 2 a.m. or later.

It was a grueling schedule, but Ghanshyam lived to help people and every consultation he did energized him. Whatever money came in went directly back into the Center to finance the palmistry school Ghanshyam was planning—his dream was to teach the world about the beauty and benefits of palmistry. He was frustrated that most North Americans thought of palmistry as fakery or fortune-telling, and he was determined to change that notion, to demystify palmistry by educating as many people as possible about its proven abilities to provide insight into our psychological makeup and help restore mental, emotional and spiritual health. I had personally witnessed and experienced this myself, so I was happy to help him in his mission.

Once a month, Ghanshyam, Kathy and Peter traveled outside of Montreal to visit clients in Boston, New York and Toronto, wherever people needed their help. I thought of Ghanshyam and his team as Santa and his elves, working feverishly around the clock preparing beautiful gifts to deliver to humanity. When they returned from their road trips, I would add a fresh pile of before-and-after prints to the archives.

I loved working in the archives and spent hours looking for prints to be used in class, studying the various features of the hand and reading about the history of the Center.

I discovered Ghanshyam had begun learning palmistry, astrology and Ayurvedic medicine when he was just a boy sitting at the side of his grandfather in the small village in India where he was born. People traveled from around the region to seek his grandfather's help, advice and the natural remedies he prepared to cure their ailments. Ghanshyam was enthralled by the accuracy and healing power of palmistry and began studying the books on Vedic sciences in his grandfather's library. He began reading the hands of his schoolmates, and before he had reached his teens, he would sneak out of the house and into the village on his own to sketch the handprints of whomever he met on the street, from policemen to prostitutes—palmistry had gotten into his blood and would become his life's great passion.

In 1953, on his 12th birthday, the family's astrologer was summoned to consult Ghanshyam's natal chart, which had been misplaced since his birth. (Astrology and palmistry were such a normal part of Indian life that having a family astrologer was quite normal.) The astrologer studied the chart carefully and announced to Ghanshyam's family that their son was destined to become a missionary of palmistry—he would travel far from home and change the way palmistry was practiced and perceived, transforming it from a method of fortune-telling to a healing art that would help many people.

Oddly enough, Ghanshyam did not like predictions. He hated how fatalistic palmistry had become over the centuries and wanted to practice it as it once had been, as his grandfather practiced it—to help and heal. And he wanted to begin practicing as soon as he finished high school, but his father, a no-nonsense army man, was against it—he thought Ghanshyam would end up broke and on the street—the same worry my own father had had when I set off to Europe.

Ghanshyam appeased his father by joining the military cadets and earning his bachelor's degree, but he continued studying palmistry and astrology in his spare time. After he graduated and became a college instructor, he also opened his first Palmistry Center in New Delhi and found a teacher who could instruct him further in the purest form of palmistry.

That teacher was Shyamlalji, a reclusive but revered palmist who refused to take on students unless they convinced him they would dedicate their lives to palmistry—which Ghanshyam did, becoming one of only two students Shyamlalji ever accepted.

Shyamlalji practiced a deeply spiritual form of palmistry and Ghanshyam followed a rigorous training program of fasting, prayer, mantra recitation, and meditation, amassing a wealth of technical knowledge and embracing palmistry's mystical and metaphysical aspects. During his training, Ghanshyam was forced to confront his inner self and became convinced palmistry could not be practiced effectively without a profound self-knowledge or continual self-analysis.

Shyamlalji also made a prediction about Ghanshyam's future similar to the one the family astrologer had made years before: "You will travel to the West and revolutionize palmistry for future generations." So when Ghanshyam saw an ad in a New Delhi newspaper searching for "the best palmist in India" to work at a restaurant in Montreal, he heard destiny calling. More than 500 palmists from across India applied, but the job went to Ghanshyam. At the time, he was newly married with young children, and his family, friends and colleagues told him he was crazy to give up his teaching career to work in a foreign restaurant, but he followed his heart. In 1970, he left India for Canada without a dime to his name or knowing a word of either official language. At customs, all he had to declare was his love of palmistry and his dream of bringing it to the world.

Ghanshyam struggled at first in Montreal, but his passion for palmistry and the accuracy of his readings quickly won him a large and loyal following. One of his most ardent supporters was the highly regarded psychologist Judy Freppel, who had been the president of the Quebec Association of Psychologists.

Like me, Judy was amazed by the detailed analysis Ghanshyam provided her simply by looking at her hands. She was so impressed with his abilities that she regularly brought her own clients, colleagues and students to him for readings.

"I spend hours and hours with my patients, trying to construct a picture of their personality," she told Ghanshyam. "But you spend just 30 minutes with them and not only do you know their personality inside and out, you identify their greatest fears and phobias, pinpoint their strengths and weaknesses, *and* provide them with sound suggestions on what they can do to resolve their problems. You teach them how to analyze their behavior and prevent them from making the same mistakes again and again."

Judy was convinced Ghanshyam's mission to introduce analytic and "preventative palmistry" to the world was so worthwhile that she left her private practice to work with him full-time. In 1972, she found a space for the office, helped set up the Palmistry Center and organized the Center's first board of directors, which included several doctors, psychologists and university professors.

Judy also shared Ghanshyam's devotion to the teachings of Paramahansa Yogananda and Kriya Yoga—so much so that, a few years later, she left the Center to become a nun at Paramahansa's ashram in California, eventually working as a private secretary to Daya Mata, the president of SRF. Ghanshyam was devastated to lose his dear friend and right-hand woman, but by that time Kathy had joined the Center.

Kathy had been studying psychology at university in Montreal, when, on her 19th birthday, she was presented with a set of books about the history and practice of palmistry. Like Ghanshyam and Judy, she immediately recognized how helpful palmistry could be for her and for others. She spent the next seven years studying it on her own and searching for a teacher or a school that could help her reach the next level and become a professional palmist. Her search ended when she met Ghanshyam in 1975, just as Judy was preparing to leave the Center.

"I'm leaving you in Kathy's capable hands—you can do nothing but succeed," Judy told Ghanshyam shortly before moving to Los Angeles.

"The two of you are going to help a lot of people and the Center will continue to grow and prosper."

And that's exactly what happened—besides conducting her own consultations and teaching classes, Kathy became the Center's official historian and dedicated herself to recording Ghanshyam's background, knowledge and lectures, from which I and many others would benefit.

The coming months were going to be very challenging for me, but after learning how the Palmistry Center was born and the sacrifices Ghanshyam made to bring Vedic palmistry to the West, I was proud to have joined this dedicated group and be part of such a worthy cause.

CHAPTER 9

My Teachers

WHILE I WAS PROUD to be a member of the Palmistry Center team, I found it difficult to shake old attitudes and habits and adjust to my new life. The work first assigned to me was not what I was accustomed to, given my former Parisian lifestyle, education and so-called glamorous television career. I spent a lot of time licking stamps and scrubbing toilets, which was not exactly the path to enlightenment I had envisioned! And while I tried to take it in stride—to keep calm, carry on and be cheery, I guess my anxiety and inner dissatisfaction seeped into my moods.

One night while working late, I overheard a conversation between Peter and Ghanshyam in an adjoining room. My English was not great, but my *Larousse English-French Dictionary* was always in my pocket and by that point I understood enough to know they were talking about me.

"How is she working out?" Ghanshyam asked Peter. "What do you think?"

"Oh, Guylaine, she's great," Peter answered. "But she gets into these moods I don't understand and they can be pretty hard to deal with."

A shiver ran down my spine realizing the negative effect my moods were having on the people around me. My dad used to chastise me for my moodiness when I was a teen and tried (unsuccessfully) to temper my emotional swings with his pranks or teasing. But I guess my moodiness had become a habit—yet another bad habit that was blocking me. So I added moodiness to the list of flaws I needed to overcome and silently thanked Peter for teaching me something I needed to learn, even if it was an accidental lesson.

Another staff member who taught me some big lessons about my behavior was my supervisor, Lydia. She had been in charge of daily operations at the Center for years and ran a very tight ship. She was a real tough cookie—high-strung and big on rules, and she did not indulge rebellious free spirits like me. My bouncy energy and need for speed unnerved her. She would jump if I appeared at her side too quickly and would loudly order me to stand back and always stay at least three feet away from her.

If I happened to wear the same color of shoes as her, she would accuse me of trying to show her up. Answering the phone before she did could be interpreted as an attempt to steal her job. She checked and rechecked every detail of my work, no matter how mundane, and she chewed me out publicly if the sinks I cleaned did not sparkle to her satisfaction. To be fair, she was hard on everyone—even Ghanshyam—but I felt she went out of her way to make me feel like a naughty schoolgirl in constant need of correction. Once, after I made a major mistake in the appointment book, she screamed at me in front of a client.

"She shouldn't treat you like that," the client whispered to me. I agreed; however, after thinking about it for a few minutes, I realized that the client would be leaving soon and Lydia and I would still be there working together—and could be for years. We had to get along. So I said to the client, "You know what, I did make a mistake and Lydia was right to point it out to me."

But after another altercation with Lydia, I had had enough. I promptly stormed into Ghanshyam's office and complained bitterly to him about the situation, which, I thought, was justifiable. He was not impressed with my petulant tone or self-righteous attitude. He gave me a long look that I could not make out. Then he very calmly said, "Guylaine, is this how you plan to become a better person? If you made a mistake you needed to be corrected and that is Lydia's job. She is your supervisor. No one is forcing you to be here, if you are not happy, you can leave anytime you like. There's the door."

It was not the answer I was anticipating, especially from Ghanshyam. I was used to his smiles and sympathy—it stung.

Oh no!

My eyes swelled with tears. I excused myself and slipped out of his office wishing I could disappear. Kathy, who was born with a beautiful, emphatic soul, saw I was upset and stopped to give me a hug when she walked by my desk.

"Don't worry, Guylaine. Tomorrow will be a better day!"

That night, as I lay in bed, I thought about what Ghanshyam had said; he was right. Nobody was forcing me to be there, but it was where I wanted to be. I was letting myself get caught up in petty personal melodramas and blaming other people for my discontentment, just as I had done with Marcel when he got sick. I was stumbling over my ego and letting my head get in the way of my quest to grow as a person. But my fears, doubts and wounded pride made me question everything. I was stuck on the same old emotional rollercoaster I had been riding for years and wondered if I should even carry on with my efforts at self-transformation—or call it a day and start from scratch somewhere else.

I did not want to face the situation. I closed my eyes and used my secret weapon, focusing on the dark spot on the inside of my forehead until I slipped away from my body and troubled mind.

One morning, not long after that, Ghanshyam greeted me with his familiar smile when I walked into his office to deliver some handprints. Then he said something I would never forget.

"To work here, you have to accept that you must work on yourself first, Guylaine. A good palmist must never project their own anxieties, fear or negativity onto a client. People come to us for our help, not for our personal problems or worries. Change is painful, but necessary. To grow as a person you must allow your ego to be pulverized until there is nothing but heart."

Once again, Ghanshyam was correct. I chose to be at the Center to grow, to change the lines of my hand and become a better person. If I still felt trapped in my own head with my old behavior, I had to find a way to shed my negative attitude as I had shed my unsupportive friends. I had given up everything I had and walked away from my career to be at the Center and I did not want to turn back. So I secretly accepted Lydia as a teacher: her aggressiveness forced me to face the personal issues and flaws I needed to address in myself. I allowed her to pulverize my ego, and she did a very good job. I will always owe her a debt of thanks for helping me grow.

I focused on fixing my flaws and developed little strategies to improve myself and develop spiritually—walking to the post office, preparing tea for a client and taking out the trash became mini pilgrimages, opportunities to talk to God—or my soul, or Infinite Source, or whatever other name felt most appropriate to describe the Divine presence within me. Instead of wondering why I was stuck running tedious errands, I focused on following a path of peace and gratitude. Even scrubbing the sink until it shone brightly enough for Lydia to see her reflection provided me with inspiration and a sense of accomplishment.

These were great life lessons—when I approached work with gratitude I found reward in any task, which made the job go faster and gave me more time to study the lines of the hand. And when I learned that the heart line is a reflection of our soul revealing the depth of our generosity and capacity to love and forgive unconditionally, I wanted mine to grow. I began practicing little acts of kindness, like buying a large container of milk every Monday morning to ensure everyone would have it for their tea and coffee during the week. Considering my meagre income, this was a big deal for me.

Later, when I was studying Vedic astrology, I discovered two things that made me smile about that period at the Center. The first was realizing that at that time I was in a Moon *dasha*. (A *dasha* is a life phase during which we are greatly affected by a particular astral body.) And during a Moon *dasha*, it is considered auspicious to donate something liquid and white on a Monday, which corresponds to the day of the Moon!

The second thing I learned was that I was not, as I had always believed, an Aries with a Leo ascendant. That meant I was not ruled by two fire planets, Mars and Sun or driven by their hot, aggressive male (yang) energy. Western astrology calculates birth charts differently and, according to Vedic astrology, I am actually Pisces with a Cancer ascendant—two water signs! It makes a world of difference, as water energy is feminine (yin) and much more patient and giving. It was the opposite of what I had always imagined myself to be—fast, strong-willed and independent–but it certainly explained my moodiness.

My new signs confused me at first, but as I kept working on repairing my flaws I began easing into the qualities that water signs are known for, and found myself becoming more tolerant and nurturing. Before I arrived at the Center, the extent of my culinary expertise was dumping a box of Kraft Dinner in a pot and setting it to boil. After working with Ghanshyam for a while, I began to learn how to cook by helping Kathy make supper every evening. Soon, I was taking much pleasure in making meals for the staff and always made them with love. As Ghanshyam once told me, everything we create in life vibrates with our emotions on a molecular level—and so I made sure every dish I whipped up for my colleagues was prepared with gratitude and appreciation.

One gorgeous summer afternoon, Kathy dropped by my desk.

"Would you like to start learning palmistry, Guylaine?" she asked.

She took me for a picnic under a willow tree beside a stream in Westmount Park (a perfect setting for a water sign!) where she gave me the first of many private tutoring sessions in Vedic palmistry and astrology.

She began by telling me that palmistry originated thousands of years ago as part of the ancient Vedic science of *Samudrik Shastra*, which translates from Sanskrit as "Ocean of Knowledge," and that knowledge was available to us in the lines and signs of the hand.

"Palmistry has been an accepted and deeply respected part of Hindu culture for so many thousands of years. It is represented by its own goddess," Kathy told me, holding up her right hand and spreading her fingers. "Her name is Mother Panchanguli. *Panch* means five and *anguli* means fingers."

She reviewed the planetary names assigned to each of the four fingers, from index to baby finger—Jupiter, Saturn, Sun and Mercury. The dime-sized "mounts" are beneath each finger and bear the same planetary name. The Mount of Venus is below the thumb; the Mounts of Mars—Mars positive and negative—are found on either side of the palm; and across from Venus, on the opposite side of the hand, we find the Mount of Moon, also known as Luna.

"Let's start by examining the thumb," Kathy said. "In Sanskrit the thumb is called *angushth*, which means 'Supreme among the fingers,' and for good reason—the thumb is the driving force of the entire hand and is a snapshot of our individuality. It is also the conscious expression of the Mount of Venus and reveals our capacity to love. The thumb's two phalanges represent our willpower and our logic—and the way we express love can depend on the strength, development and interplay of our logic and will."

In those early sessions, my English was still a challenge, but Kathy was such a naturally gifted teacher she bypassed any language barrier by using imagery that fired my imagination and locked the information into my memory.

"Our fingers reveal a lot about us," she continued. "Short fingers with a strong Mars but not enough support from Saturn tell us that even though we have lots of energy and dynamism, we need more discernment, wisdom and discipline to reach our goals. Think of short fingers as a boat with a powerful motor but no rudder. Our energy needs direction to get us to where we want to go.

"But long fingers are another story—with a strong Saturn finger that doesn't have enough support from Mars it can be difficult to put our thoughts into action. We are like a boat with a rudder, but no motor and need to cultivate more energy in order to realize our dreams and objectives."

Kathy knew I was from a city of boats; she could not have picked a better analogy.

To explain the role of the mounts, she told me to imagine them as hydroelectric power plants. "The mounts pull in power from the planets and generate the electricity flowing through your major and minor lines. They light up your consciousness!"

She used other colorful metaphors to explain the significance of each zodiac sign and the attributes of the nine planets and the astrological houses in which they reside. She taught me how important it was to compare both hands, because together they are an expression of our conscious and subconscious. And she taught me what to look for to detect negative behavior patterns or character traits—an excellent tool for preventing old habits from resurfacing and undermining us.

Kathy literally brought palmistry home to me; with her help, I recognized how my family's hands and astrological signs were testimonies to their different personalities. I could connect my brother André's chaotic energy and misadventures to his unusually short Saturn finger. The birth chart of my brother Gaston—the great storyteller of the family who loved to talk all night—revealed he had Mercury exalted in Virgo in his second house, which, Kathy informed me, was the house of voice and communication.

Dad's prominent Sun line gave him his sunny disposition and desire to be of service to his family; his lack of Moon explained his difficulty expressing emotions—like when he could not bring himself to come to the airport to wish me farewell when I left for Paris. And my mom's strong Moon in Leo explained why she adored people so much and could happily work double shifts as a waitress—people were her passion. Her strong head line made her an excellent psychologist: she could get everyone in the family to do what was best for them. I remembered the time she got Dad to stop drinking by knocking over all the furniture after he had passed out on the couch. When he woke up in the morning, he thought he was responsible for the havoc and never touched another drop.

My own hand showed a wide separation between my life and head lines, which accounted for my independent streak and why I was the only member of my family ever to leave Valleyfield and make a home elsewhere.

Kathy's humor and passion brought palmistry to life for me, and proved to me that understanding the lines and signs of our hand could help us transform our lives and achieve our dreams.

Whenever she taught a group class, I took a front row seat so I could pepper her with questions. I was in awe of her ability to communicate complex ideas and concepts with incredible ease and eloquence. It was like watching Jimmy Hendrix play guitar—using his instrument as though it were an extension of his body, forward, backward or upside down, it did not matter—the music he created was miraculous and thrilling. It was the same with Kathy and palmistry, she lived and breathed it and taught it in a way that was electrifying. She reminded me of Obelix, one of the protagonists of the comic book series *Asterix*, who fell into a vat of magic potion as a baby and was imbued with superhuman strength: Kathy fell in the potion of palmistry, and I wanted that potion, too.

Thursday nights were reserved for Ghanshyam's weekly class. I was consistently astonished by the depth and breadth of his knowledge—he was like an archaeologist, just when I thought he had produced the most precious treasure imaginable, he would dig deeper and pull out another gem. During one class, he moved from the significance of fingernail size and shape to the importance of skin texture to the role reincarnation plays in the palm to how the energy of the universal five elements—air, water, fire, earth and ether—interact with our three levels of consciousness.

He had an encyclopedic understanding of every facet of palmistry and I made sure that I was never without my trusty English–French dictionary whenever his class was in session.

My desire to absorb every word Ghanshyam uttered when he taught made learning English a top priority and I worked on my language skills every day—and every Friday night, when the gang went out for pizza together. Even though I could not always keep up with the conversation and did not get all the jokes, I laughed a lot during those get-togethers and forged enduring friendships. Years later, Ghanshyam told me that learning palmistry in a language other than my mother tongue slowed me down and forced me to breathe more deeply, making me calmer and more capable of self-reflection—a must for any palmist.

But keeping calm did not always come easily to me. I remember breaking down in tears after a frustrating day and, of course, Kathy offered her shoulder to cry on.

"Come on now, it's not that bad. Let's have a look at what your hands have to say," she said, leading me to the sink and inking my palms. It was the first set of handprints I had taken since starting at the Center. I was so happy at what I saw, my tears were instantly forgotten—I was astounded at how much and how quickly my lines had transformed!

The first thing I noticed was the change in the overall shape of my hands and fingers: they did not look anywhere near as crooked as they had at my first session with Ghanshyam. Kathy pointed out that my thumb had opened up, showing that my self-confidence was growing. Then I saw small wisdom lines were starting to appear in my palm, particularly a Ring of Solomon, which meant I was ready to learn from a mentor and help people through my profession. Also, a new love-of-truth line was growing on my Mount of Saturn—revealing that I was learning to accept criticism and advice without being defensive or judgmental.

But, most importantly to me, my heart line had started to grow, which meant I was becoming more loving and ready to be loved—and that I was in the right place to do both.

Working at the Center opened my heart and my whole outlook on life had vastly improved: I was more positive about the future, far less moody, kinder and increasingly thoughtful of others. The change was so profound that my parents wanted to find out what was happening to me—they wanted to meet Ghanshyam.

Mom and Dad dropped by the Center a little over a year after I had started working there. Ghanshyam welcomed them in his traditional, loving fashion—with endearing humility, hearty handshakes, his irresistible smile and big hugs all around. My parents were instantly smitten and Dad and Ghanshyam began teasing each other like a couple of old school chums, which amazed me because they could not understand a word they were saying to each other. Dad spoke French in his thickest Quebecois dialect and Ghanshyam spoke in English, but they sat in the office and laughed for an hour. Mom adored Kathy and Peter and wanted to know all about their background and what had brought them to palmistry and what made our lines change.

Before they left, I took my parents handprints. While I was rolling the ink across their palms, I said a prayer of thanks for how blessed I was to have two loving families in one lifetime.

Over time, I grew more self-assured in my knowledge of palmistry. I was drawing up the astrological charts for clients before their consultations, discussing details of daily horoscopes with Peter, and helping Kathy and Ghanshyam organize and prepare their classes. I knew my dream of speaking English had been achieved when Ghanshyam appeared in my dreams and delivered messages to me—in English!

"Guylaine, be a flag, not an exhibition!" he said in one dream. I got his meaning immediately. He was instructing me to be free and shine, to feel beautiful and express myself, but also reminding me that I was channeling a vast ocean of consciousness and must not become proud or identify with ego. In another dream, he said,

"When you serve someone tea, it is not the tea you are serving but your attitude!"

Ghanshyam was as wise in my dreams as he was in person, and those two dreams gave me the courage and confidence to leave my *Larousse English–French Dictionary* in my desk drawer instead of carrying it in my pocket.

After working at the Center for two years, I was fluent enough in both English and palmistry to travel with the team to Toronto, where they were conducting consultations at a huge esoteric trade show. Thousands of people attended the weekend-long event and I was in charge of organizing the readings, arranging our accommodations and making sure the consultations ran smoothly. But, on the second day of the trade show, one of the palmists fell sick, and Ghanshyam turned to me.

"Okay Guylaine, you're up! It's your turn to do a consultation. You are ready. You can do it—you've done so many in the past!"

In the past? What past? What was he talking about? Reincarnation?

I had never done a consultation before—not ever, at least not in this lifetime. I wanted to tell Ghanshyam to find someone else, but he did not give me the chance. And there wasn't any time to protest, there was only a situation that needed to be immediately resolved—a client was waiting for his reading and others were lining up behind him.

Ghanshyam nodded toward the empty chair. I focused my breath to still my trembling hands and sat down in front of my first client. He placed his hand on the table and I began to analyze his lines. It was a short reading, maybe 15 or 20 minutes, but it felt like an eternity.

When it was over, he stood up and smiled, nodding.

"Thank you," he said. "What you told me made a *lot* of sense to me."

He thanked me again, and left—my first satisfied customer.

I looked over at Ghanshyam; he gave me a thumbs-up. In that beautiful moment, my career as a professional palmist was launched.

CHAPTER 10

Paramahansa Yogananda

*I*WAS GRATEFUL FOR ALL my teachers at the Center, and especially grateful for finding a mentor as wise and caring as Ghanshyam, who called me on my behavior and did not allow me to be my own worst enemy. And I was grateful that Ghanshyam had chosen Paramahansa Yogananda as both his teacher and his guru.

Paramahansa Yogananda may have died in 1952, but his spirit and teachings were very much alive in his books and through the Self-Realization Fellowship he founded to carry on his work.

In the evenings, I reread chapters of *Autobiography of a Yogi* and was constantly inspired by the many powerful student-teacher (disciple–guru) relationships described in those fascinating pages. Especially the relationships between Paramahansa and his enlightened guru, Sri Yukteswar Giri; Sri Yukteswar's relationship with his own guru, Lahiri Mahasaya; and Lahiri's relationship with *his* guru, Mahavatar Babaji.

Lahiri was an accountant but he was also a deeply spiritual man searching for God. His life was forever changed when he encountered Babaji while hiking along a lonely mountain path in the Himalayas in 1861. Babaji, as a fully God-realized being, defies both human understanding and the laws of space and time, materializing or dematerializing at will. Some believe he has lived in human form for thousands of years and has guided many prophets in their missions—and he had a mission for Lahiri: to reintroduce Kriya Yoga to the world.

In *Autobiography,* Kriya Yoga is described as an ancient and closely guarded science that allows the devoted practitioner to realize God through special yogic meditation that energizes the body, stimulates the chakras and awakens the "third eye," or Christ Consciousness. Kriya Yoga was originally discovered by enlightened sages in India millennia ago; it is derived from inspired writings in the sacred Vedic texts and recorded in the Yoga Sutras. Lord Krishna praised the practice of Kriya Yoga in the *Bhagavad Gita,* the Hindu Bible, and some say Kriya Yoga was known to Jesus and his disciples. But knowledge of Kriya Yoga was lost to history during the Dark Ages and completely forgotten about for centuries.

Babaji initiated Lahiri in Kriya Yoga and instructed him to pass on the Kriya Yoga "key" only to those truly seeking God. Lahiri taught Kriya Yoga to Sri Yukteswar, who gave it to Paramahansa. It was ordained by Babaji that Kriya Yoga be brought to the West by Paramahansa, which he did when he sailed from India to America in 1920. He founded the Self-Realization Fellowship in California to bridge the wide philosophical gap separating Eastern and Western spirituality and to make Kriya Yoga accessible to anyone earnestly searching to know God, no matter what their religion, creed or nationality.

Everyone at the Center followed Paramahansa's teachings and practiced Kriya Yoga—and I would learn that thousands of others in North America did as well, including many famous personalities, such as Greta Garbo, George Harrison and Elvis Presley, as did Mahatma Gandhi, who was instructed in Kriya Yoga by Paramahansa himself. The amazing saga of Kriya Yoga's emergence in Western culture is chronicled on the cover of The Beatles' *Sgt. Pepper* album, which features the faces and direct lineage of the Kriya Yoga gurus: Babaji, Lahiri, Sri Yukteswar and Paramahansa.

I especially related to Lahiri's story in *Autobiography* because, even though he was God-realized and could perform miraculous feats, he continued to work at his day job and remained a good husband and father to his five children. It was reassuring to me that one did not have to live in an ashram or move to a Himalayan cave to find God; regular working people could find Him too, provided they searched faithfully with an open heart and mind. And according to the wisdom of saints and sages in *Autobiography* (and Ghanshyam, too!) the fastest and most effective way to open our mind and heart to God is through meditation and the regular practice of Kriya Yoga.

I was determined to incorporate Kriya Yoga into my life. But first, I had to practice the special exercises established by Paramahansa. When the SRF lessons I had sent away for after my first sessions with Ghanshyam arrived, I practiced the recommended energization exercises every morning and most evenings. Ghanshyam was right about them not being a mere fitness routine—they really did direct positive cosmic energy into my spine. The more I practiced, the less I felt driven by my nervous energy—my spine straightened and my breathing grew deeper and more relaxed.

The SRF lessons also included a concentration exercise called *Hong-Sau*, which helped me focus on searching for what I was looking for—becoming a better person—and avoiding emotional distractions and mood swings. I also started practicing meditation, beginning with the technique provided in the lessons known as *Aum* meditation. *Aum* is described in *Autobiography* as the primal creative force, a "vibration that reverberates throughout the universe." I felt that positive vibration rise in me whenever I sat quietly and allowed the beautiful sound to echo in my mind.

Once I began meditating, I never wanted to go "into the black" or leave my body again. I realized my secret weapon had been a needed but temporary way to escape my unhappiness, but my misery would always be there in the morning. In meditation, I was able to dissolve my sadness and anxiety and replace these with a calmness and peace that stayed with me throughout the day. Meditation did not make my problems or my "12 flaws" disappear, but it sure helped me to put them into perspective and start dealing with them. Meditating was like laying a spiritual foundation in preparation for receiving joy.

Practicing the energization exercises and the *Hong-Sau* and *Aum* meditation techniques is a prerequisite for receiving Kriya Yoga "initiation" from the SRF, the only organization sanctioned by Paramahansa to teach Kriya Yoga. It is considered such a powerful spiritual tool that at least a full year of preparatory work is required before a candidate is deemed ready to receive the technique. It is like training for a marathon or a mountain climb—you have to work toward it slowly or you could hurt yourself.

Initiation into Kriya Yoga is offered to students once a year at special ceremonies in selected cities, during which an ordained SRF Minister performs *diksha* on the initiate—a spiritual baptism intended to awaken the third eye in the center of the forehead through a hands-on transference of Divine energy. It is a great blessing for those setting out on their journey to find God and receiving it was very important to me.

I completed my lessons in 12 months, just in time for that year's initiation ceremony in Toronto. Ghanshyam, Peter, Kathy and the rest of the gang piled into two cars and drove to Toronto with me to lend their support and celebrate afterward. We arrived the evening before the event and I lined up with scores of other initiates to register.

"I'm sorry," the clerk at the desk said when it was my turn to register, "but your name is not on the list."

Apparently, because I had started my lessons in French and then switched to English when my language skills improved, my name had been lost in red tape and paperwork.

"You'll have to wait another year to be initiated."

It was a devastating blow—I had worked so hard and waited so long to reach this starting point, it pained me to put my journey on hold. Ghanshyam and Kathy told me to meditate and not to worry—and they went to see Brother Ramananda, the senior Monk conducting the ceremony that weekend, and asked him as a personal favor to allow me to be initiated. His hands were tied, he told them. Unless he received the proper approval from SRF headquarters in Los Angeles by first thing the next morning, I would have to wait a year.

That night, I dreamed of Lahiri Mahasaya, who had received Kriya Yoga from Babaji more than a century earlier on that Himalayan mountaintop and whom I considered the working man's guru. In my dream, Lahiri approached me carrying three bars of chocolate on his shoulders—two bars were quite small and the third was enormous—and he gave me all three. Even in my dream I understood that the two small bars represented the *Hong-Sau* and the *Aum* techniques; the large chocolate bar represented Kriya Yoga. I awoke in the morning knowing I was going to be initiated that day. When I arrived at the ceremony, Brother Ramananda smiled, said he had just received the necessary permission and welcomed me with open arms.

The ceremony had a solemnity and beauty that brought tears to my eyes. When the Minister touched my forehead and performed *diksha*, my spine began to tingle and I felt I was drifting toward heaven—the weight of years of accumulated doubt, fear, insecurity and anxiety slid from my shoulders.

I had been struggling to change; now I felt I could. It was a new beginning.

CHAPTER 11

Family Spirit

*I*RETURNED FROM THE ESOTERIC trade show in Toronto feeling triumphant—after two years of studying palmistry, I had done my first consultation and was officially a palmist. I was a rookie, for sure, and had years of learning ahead of me—but still, I was a palmist and it felt wonderful. After that first reading—which I had done in English!—my blockages and fears began melting away. I was ready to move to the next level and use my skills to be of service to others.

Ghanshyam suggested I start off by conducting short consultations at local street festivals where the Center would set up booths. Heading into the streets of Montreal to begin my new career was exhilarating—I remember first arriving in the city with big dreams of making it in the television industry, which left me feeling soulless and uninspired. Now, I was in the business of inspiring souls and helping people achieve their dreams.

The street festivals were colorful and crowded and I loved being surrounded by so many unread palms—each hand filled with unique challenges and potential, and each an opportunity to learn and to help.

My first client, a young woman whom I will refer to as Suzette, was in her early 20s with a rectangular, conic hand, which suggested she may be artistically inclined and more governed by emotions than practicalities. She had a thatch of crisscrossing lines cutting off and blocking each other, which made me suspect there was a lot of conflict and stress in her life. Her Sun finger was small and leaning on her Saturn, which told me she lacked self-confidence and felt insecure in herself and her accomplishments—feelings I had been all too familiar with in my life.

It was only a 15-minute session, and I wanted to focus on the most positive aspects her hand presented.

"Look at this beautiful Girdle of Venus," I said, directing her attention to the lovely, semicircular line looping between her Saturn and Sun fingers, like a sweet smile atop her troubled palm.

"This tells me you are very creative, but some of your other lines indicate you could be having difficulty expressing it."

Suzette nodded and told me I was right: she was an art student but felt like it was taking her nowhere and she was thinking about quitting. She wanted a longer consultation and booked a few appointments to see me at the Center, making her my first regular client.

My career was taking off more quickly that I could have imagined or hoped. Luckily, I always had Ghanshyam and Kathy to rely on for guidance and support when I needed to discuss a complicated print or chart. Their expertise, caring and assurance gave me the courage and confidence I needed to come into my own. Even so, to this day I still feel a twinge of anxiety whenever I sit down with a client. My legs get all tied up in knots under my desk, but I never let my nervousness show on my face. I have learned to trust what the lines tell me, and that my racing heart is a sign of excitement, not fear. Once a consultation is underway, I relax into the reading, my legs untangle and I am happy to be of service and able to enjoy myself. And when I see people leave feeling better than when they arrived, with a better understanding of themselves, I am elated. That is when I see the miracle of palmistry in action.

I had that feeling after my follow-up consultations with Suzette. When she came into the Center, her handprints reaffirmed her powerful creative energy as well as the blockages and low self-esteem. And her birth chart revealed conflicts in the houses relating to family.

"My parents always favored my sister—to them, she could do no wrong. But anything I do is never good enough, not even my artwork."

Suzette considered herself a failure and planned to drop out of art school, marry a man her parents disapproved of and support herself working at odd jobs.

I looked closer at her Sun line and saw a large star on it, which indicated a potential for great success if she followed her passion—which was her art. We talked about how she perceived the world, setting goals to channel her energy and how she could best pursue her passion. After a couple of readings she decided to stay in school for another year until she found a rewarding job as a graphic designer. Six months into her series of readings, the lines on her palm had changed and improved.

Suzette's reading reminded me of something Ghanshyam had said during one of our first sessions—that palmistry is about prevention and positive change. And to make positive changes and prevent life from beating us down or sidetracking our dreams, it was essential to surround ourselves with loving, positive and supportive friends and family—the kind of supportive friends I had made at the Center, who were now family to me.

Kathy and Peter often invited me to their parents' house for dinner and Mr. and Mrs. Keogh welcomed me into their hearts and home as though I were a long-lost daughter. The house was always filled with people, food and music, with Frank Sinatra crooning in the background. Like my dad, Mr. Keogh had a great sense of humor and Mrs. Keogh could not have been sweeter or more supportive. She always told me I looked beautiful and encouraged me to pursue my dream of becoming a palmist. Kathy and Peter's sister, Anne-Marie, and brother, Brian, also treated me as one of the family and we became good friends.

Some Sundays, the only day the Center was closed, we would go over to Ghanshyam's house and enjoy a delicious Indian feast prepared by his wife, Chanchala, and have fun with their three children.

But one of my favorite get-togethers was bringing my two families together when Ghanshyam, Kathy, Peter and I would drive down to Valleyfield to visit my parents and Mom would make us her special chicken and vegetable dish. The English–French barrier was never a problem around the table because we ended up laughing more than talking. After dinner we would head to the basement to play bean bag toss, which Kathy, who had impressive powers of concentration, usually won handily.

During my first years practicing palmistry, I relied on the strong bonds I had formed with my family at the Center when tragedy befell my Valleyfield family.

In late 1986, my father was diagnosed with esophageal cancer—but he never knew it. Dad feared cancer so much and had such a sensitive and emotional nature that the doctor and my mother agreed that if he were aware of the extent of his illness he would see it as the end of the line and give up. Dad only knew he had a mass in his throat and needed to undergo treatment to have it removed.

Soon after the diagnosis, Mom and Dad came to the Center for their very first consultation with Ghanshyam. Dad was in good spirits when he arrived and my English was good enough by then for me to sit in on the session to translate. I was amazed at how much my father had come to appreciate palmistry. He had witnessed the radical improvement it had made in my life and he admired and respected Ghanshyam and his work. Dad and Ghanshyam usually joked together when they saw each other, but not this time. When Dad sat down for his consultation, he was as serious as when he sat in church and listened reverently to everything Ghanshyam had to say.

"You are a true artist in your work, Lionel, a real craftsman," Ghanshyam told him, studying Dad's handprints and chart. "And you are a very hard worker—you could have been a successful independent contractor if circumstances had permitted, instead of working for other people."

Dad had retired by then and appreciated the validation of his skill. He was extremely artistic in his carpentry and had built many beautiful houses over the years. If he had not been so dedicated to providing for his family since he was a boy, I am sure he would have started his own business and have been hugely successful.

"This line here is an assistant to the life line, it provides you with a lot of support and stamina," Ghanshyam said. He looked up and pointed to my mother. "That assistance comes from your wife, and you need to listen to her."

Dad laughed. Mom had always been his greatest supporter, and she constantly prodded him to eat better and tried to improve his health by feeding him vegetables—which, as a meat-and-potatoes man, he always resisted.

After the reading, Ghanshyam took Mom aside.

"Please, Laurette, I know this is breaking your heart, but don't cry in front of him. And at night, don't let yourself imagine him being dead. He sleeps next to you and he will sense what you are thinking—he is very, very sensitive and it could weaken him. But if you think and act positively, he will live longer, and I know you want him with you as long as possible."

Mom hugged Ghanshyam and took his advice to heart. No matter how sick Dad became in the coming months, she never treated him like an invalid and did everything possible to keep his spirits up. When she noticed he was losing weight, she would get up in the middle of the night with her needle and thread and secretly take in the waist of every pair of pants he owned. When he stepped onto the bathroom scale, she discreetly placed her foot behind him to add a few pounds to the readout. Months later, when I took Dad's handprints again, his assistant to the life line had grown considerably, thanks to Mom's efforts!

And maybe Ghanshyam's efforts, too. After my parents' consultation, Ghanshyam asked Dad if he would build a desk for the reception area. It was a sweet gesture that touched my heart; I could see Ghanshyam was looking for ways to keep Dad busy and keep his mind off his illness. And, of course, Dad built an incredibly gorgeous desk that elegantly concealed all the office phones, fax machines and printers, and it still graces the Palmistry Center to this day. Once the desk was installed, Ghanshyam found other projects for Dad to work on, including a desk for Kathy, which was so beautiful she said it made her feel like a princess.

About a year after my father's diagnosis, I woke up feeling extremely nauseous. It was January 18, 1988, and I remember the morning as vividly as if it were yesterday. I went to work, but by the afternoon I was feeling worse and my right eyelid began fluttering. According to one branch of Vedic astrology, a fluttering left eyelid in women is a good omen, while a fluttering right eyelid is a cautionary sign that there's a difficult situation on the horizon that we need to prepare for.

That afternoon Mom called me at the office.

"Guylaine, are you sitting down? I have bad news."

"What's happened, Mom?"

"It's Normand—he's dead."

Normand drove a huge transport truck and had had a heart attack while on the road. He managed to pull onto the shoulder to avoid hitting other vehicles and then slumped over the steering wheel, dead. He was 36 years old.

My stomach churned—my heart was breaking for my sister Mimi, who had been deeply in love with Normand since they had met when I was in my teens. He was such a great guy. I remembered how he had promised to—and did—smooth things over between Dad and me when I moved to Paris, and how devoted he was to Mimi and their children. He was considerate and selfless to the end—the last thing he did in life was to protect others by turning his vehicle off the road before he died.

Now he was gone, and Mimi was a widow at 32 with two young children to raise—seven-year-old Danny and two-year-old Jessica, who was just learning to talk. It seemed so unfair; I could not bear the thought of my sister suffering and rushed to Valleyfield to be with her.

Mimi was crying desperately, and we were all there to support her. Later, I went to collect baby Jessie, who was being cared for by a neighbor. I bundled her in her snowsuit and carried her home. Along the way back, she looked up at the night sky and said in her sweet little voice, "Look, Aunt Guylaine! The stars are talking to us!"

"Yes, Jessie, the stars are talking to us, and so is your daddy," I answered through my tears. I squeezed her tightly, wanting to protect her from the hardship she was about to face.

At the funeral, two dozen of Normand's coworkers pulled into the cemetery in their big 18-wheeler trucks; when he was laid to rest, they bid him farewell by blasting their horns in unison. The sound echoed above us like a hundred blaring trumpets and could be heard miles away. It sent chills up our spines, this brotherhood joining together to mourn one of their own. Everyone burst into tears. Poor Mimi was inconsolable. At the luncheon afterward, Ghanshyam took her hand in his to comfort her.

"Don't worry, Mimi," he said softly, glancing at her palm, "someone will come into your life to help you."

Mimi kissed him on the cheek and rushed away. We were all shocked that he would say that—it hardly seemed to be the appropriate time or place. But I now know my sister needed strength and hope to get through that day, and Ghanshyam saw that hope clearly in the lines of her palm and had to tell her so. And he was correct; a few years later, someone did come into Mimi's life and made her very happy.

After Normand's death, Dad's condition began to deteriorate. In the fall of 1988, he was admitted into a Montreal hospital for a month. I visited him every night and massaged his feet. He would wait for me with the bottle of mustard oil and, when we were done, he would introduce me to his new friends. He knew all the patients, and told them his corny jokes to get them laughing. He must have been terrified of what he was going through himself, but it was just like Dad to make sure those around him did not lose heart and felt better about their own problems.

One night, as I massaged the mustard oil into his feet, he looked up at me with great tenderness and said, "Guylaine, I love you."

"Me too, Dad. Me too."

On the way home that night, I broke into tears on the bus. Dad could never express himself in words, but he had always shown his love for us through his actions—providing for us no matter what it cost him personally. Hearing him articulate his love for me when he was at his lowest was overwhelming—his spirit was so much stronger than mine.

A few weeks later, I was at the Center preparing our Christmas mailing when Mimi called from Valleyfield.

"Dad's just been taken to the hospital. He isn't doing well at all, Guylaine."

I understood what that meant and left immediately. The entire family was at Dad's beside when I arrived. He looked so small and vulnerable, but he was happy I was there and smiled at me weakly when I took his hand. He asked if I could give him some candy, but as I turned to get him a piece, my brother Réjean gently placed his hand on my arm.

"He can't swallow anything," he whispered, "he's scheduled for surgery tomorrow morning to have a tube inserted in his throat. It's permanent; from now on he'll be fed through a tube."

Oh God! What a horrid way to live! I buried my face into Réjean's shoulder. Dad loved life, food and talking too much to go on living that way. Thank goodness he never had to; he passed away in his sleep that night.

We buried him on December 23rd and celebrated Christmas Eve the next night, for the sake of the grandchildren and because that is what Dad would have wanted. While we were exchanging gifts, Gaston opened a present Dad had left him beneath the Christmas tree. It was a fur glove with a strip of plastic sewn onto the end to scrape ice from a car's windshield. Dad had wrapped it to make it look like a furry animal trying to crawl out of the box. We all broke out laughing, and crying. It was typical Lionel humor and we already missed him terribly.

But he was there with us, in spirit and in every bit of brick and wood he had used to build our home. For years after he passed, Mom kept finding little gifts and love notes he had hidden for her in nooks and crannies. One note read: "Just because I am gone, don't think I am not always with you."

It was exactly what I thought during the drive back to Montreal after the holidays. I remembered the little house Dad had built for me in our backyard in Lancaster when I was two years old. I always carried the happiness that little house gave in my heart, and now I would always carry Dad there as well.

CHAPTER 12

The Art of Palmistry

LOSING TWO FAMILY MEMBERS in less than a year was a painful reminder of how little time we have to express our love and achieve our dreams. I loved practicing palmistry, and dreamed of mastering it, but the more I studied, the more I appreciated its vastness and complexity. And as I approached 30, I wondered if one lifetime was enough to realize my dream.

Then Ghanshyam said something that made me examine my approach to palmistry and to life—and gave me a new perspective on both.

"If you want to be an excellent palmist, you have to walk, sleep and breathe palmistry. It must become part of you. Just like an artist who is in love with his art, you have to develop a great focus on this love of palmistry."

His words hit their mark; I would live a life dedicated to the art of palmistry, and I would make every moment count. The next several years were ones of rapid personal and professional growth—both for me and the Center.

To remain focused on my objective, I began what has become a lifelong love affair with daily mantra meditation. Ghanshyam taught me how to recite the Gayatri Mantra, with its ageless beauty that can tap into the Divine and revitalize every cell in the body. I called upon it whenever my thoughts wandered. I have probably recited 100,000 mantras over the years while in line at the supermarket, on the bus or sitting in a dentist chair—perfect opportunities to convert idle or wasteful time into moments of peace and personal development.

To gain a greater understanding of the spiritual roots of *hast jyotish*, I began reading ancient Vedic texts: the *Ramayana*, the *Mahabharata* and Paramahansa's translation of the *Bhagavad Gita*. The inspired wisdom woven through those epic stories kept me up nights pondering the duality of existence, the frailty of human nature and the nobility of the human spirit.

I threw myself into my work, taking classes with Ghanshyam and Kathy at every opportunity and doing more and more consultations, slowly creating my own list of regular clients. My passion for palmistry grew with each passing week and I was usually at the Center more often than I was at home, and many nights I did not go home at all. In quiet recognition of my dedication, Ghanshyam had a shower and small dressing room built at the Center, which I both appreciated and made frequent use of on nights when I worked or studied until dawn.

Some of my clients were so fascinated by palmistry's uncanny ability to identify their character traits and motivations that I ended up spending more time explaining to them how palm reading works than reading their palms. But they did not mind, and neither did I—in fact, I loved teaching palmistry and wanted to do more.

At Ghanshyam's suggestion, I started teaching an Introduction to Palmistry class and later, to my delight, I was able to team up with Kathy, my teaching idol. We formed a bilingual tag team— she would teach a class in English during the week on a specific feature of the hand, then I would teach the same class in French on Saturday morning. We did an entire series that way; it was a huge hit with clients and became quite an event.

The classes always filled to capacity but were very intimate— students bonded with one another, swapping phone numbers and socializing. One began bringing a guitar and everyone would sing before class, and each student would bring a tasty treat to share with the others. Denise Parisé, who held a top position at an international accounting firm, faithfully brought doughnuts every Saturday, never missing a class—except once. It was a seminar on Saturn and I did not want her to fall behind. When I called to give her some catch-up notes, she burst into tears.

"Oh, Guylaine, I'm sorry. I love learning about palmistry, but I had to work. I hate my job. I don't know what to do!"

"Denise, I understand how you feel," I told her. "Come and see Ghanshyam. He helped me and I'm sure he can help you."

Denise booked several sessions with Ghanshyam and, in the process, she became one of our star pupils, never missing another class. Before I knew it, she quit her high-paying job and was happily working (for peanuts, like the rest of us) at the Center. A few months later, Ghanshyam had a similar life-changing impact on Johanne Riopel, a professional translator who had studied palmistry as a teen but had put it aside once she went to university. Like Denise, she had career success but was unhappy. After a few sessions with Ghanshyam in Toronto, she moved to Montreal and reconnected with her love of palmistry. She enrolled in all our palmistry classes and soon joined our little family at the Center.

Ghanshyam established the Birla College of Vedic Palmistry at the Center in 1975 and we were constantly adding to the curriculum. We worked hard developing a university-level program that would one day be recognized by the Government of Canada and that ensured graduates were prepared for careers as professional palmists—the only program of its kind outside of India.

Teaching had never originally been an ambition of mine, but practicing palmistry and meditation were creating new neural pathways in my brain and I was discovering hidden talents. Nothing gave me more satisfaction or pride than seeing that spark of understanding ignite in a student's eyes when they grasped palmistry's potential to change lives and recognized its subtle, elegant beauty.

But I don't think anyone was prouder than my mother, who came to one of my Saturday morning classes during a visit to Montreal. She beamed at me from the front row and I could see my own happiness reflected in her smiling face.

"You are living my dream, my sweet girl!" Mom told me later. "Guylaine, you are a born teacher; you inspire everyone." Her support meant the world to me. She had dreamed of being a teacher herself and probably would have if she had been given the opportunity. Now she took every opportunity to come to the city and see me teach.

"I don't always understand what you are talking about when you're up there," she told me, "but what you say makes me feel so good I am recharged for the whole week!"

Mom—with her long head line—was bright and intuitive and understood more than she let on, a fact confirmed by my sister.

"Mom's teaching all the neighbors about palmistry now," Mimi told me over the phone from Valleyfield, amused by my mother's keenness.

Our classes were in such demand that Kathy and I decided to take them on the road. We began teaching in libraries across the region—again, I handled the French sessions and Kathy taught in English. The classes became as popular with the general public as they were at the Center. It was an odd subject for the library crowd, but once we broke the ice and made a personal connection by reading a few palms, the audiences were as awed as we were by what palmistry can tell us about ourselves.

Once, when there was an oversight in our appointment book, our receptionist burst into my office while I was in the middle of a consultation.

"Guylaine! The library just phoned. They have a huge crowd and everyone is waiting for *you*!"

Oops!

I was tied up with private readings that night and because the seminar was in French, Kathy could not fill in for me. So we recruited Johanne, the fledgling Birla team member. It would be baptism by fire, but we had total confidence in her—Johanne possessed a remarkably flexible thumb, making her open and adaptable—and she had a strong Mercury line, the sign of a great communicator. Kathy briefed her on the prints she would need and then sent Johanne running to the library, where she performed brilliantly.

We were attracting more clients and students and were in need of more space, so Ghanshyam invested everything he had to expand the Center. Originally, it was a two-story building, but Ghanshyam, who has the spatulate hands and fingertips of a visionary to whom no dream is too big, added a third floor and commissioned plans to construct an amphitheater for large lectures and public seminars.

Unfortunately, the building had hidden structural damage requiring extensive (and expensive) repair and the amphitheater had to be dismantled. Three floors provided plenty of room to increase the size of our palmistry and astrology classes and offer workshops in yoga, meditation, gemology and numerology. We also set up a library of Vedic and esoteric texts and a handprint gallery to display our most notable prints. We had accumulated an amazingly varied collection—each a glimpse into an extraordinary life, from child prodigies, to victims of violence and abuse, to aristocrats to farmers and movie stars. We had a print to illustrate almost any situation and circumstance, an invaluable teaching resource. We also expanded beyond the building, and beyond Quebec—opening our first branch office in Toronto with the help of Pasquali Roberto, one of our good clients, to boost our presence in English Canada.

It was an exciting time. We were touching many lives, but we wanted to touch many more and fulfill Ghanshyam's dream of introducing Vedic palmistry across North America. We knew that goal would not be achieved by word of mouth alone or on the library circuit—we needed to broaden our reach. I could now draw upon my experience in the television industry and put it to good use. At that time, television was the best medium to reach a wide audience so we decided to take our message to the airwaves. We called every local and network station in Montreal and pitched our idea for a program about palmistry. It was a novel concept and I was certain some bright young producer would eventually pick it up.

Our first big break came in 1992, when Quebec cable giant Videotron agreed to air a 13-show series we called Être bien dans *sa peau* (Feeling Comfortable in Your Own Skin). It was, to put it gently, a low-budget affair—no makeup artist, no assistants, no crew and no set. There was a bare room, a desk with a black curtain backdrop, one camera, a part-time camera operator, and me. Videotron reached a huge audience and it was our launching pad into mainstream media—an opportunity to touch thousands of lives and we planned to make the most of it.

The segments were taped early in the morning and I had arrived at Kathy's place as the sun was coming up. She helped me pick out an outfit from her closet and do my hair and makeup while I munched toast and went over the script and prints with her. Before I rushed out the door, Kathy gave me an encouraging hug and some sage advice.

"Let the handprints speak for themselves; each line has a story and you are there to tell that story."

I would jump on the Number 24 bus and head to the studio with my stack of handprints, feeling a little out of place among the morning commuters with my heavily painted, camera-ready face.

There was some occasional nervousness in the studio, especially when the cameraman left me alone with the camera running to go work on another show, but I followed Kathy's advice: I let the handprints speak for themselves. And they did, beautifully.

Each 30-minute show had a specific theme and we used before-and-after prints of friends and clients to illustrate how dramatically our lines can change when we change our thoughts and actions. In one episode entitled "Is Your Head Line Your Best Friend or Your Worst Enemy?," Kathy and Peter's father volunteered his prints as an example of how we can make our head line grow. In some cases, a short head line can mean we are letting fear and insecurity prevent us from exploring our full potential. A longer head line, especially in a balanced hand, shows we have found the courage and conviction to pursue our dreams.

Mr. Keogh was a musician in his youth and had a very creative spirit, but he worked as a salesman most of his adult life to support his family. The prints we took before he retired revealed a very short head line. However, in retirement he pursued many creative activities—he took French lessons, began writing, and took up pottery, just to name a few—and his "after retirement prints" showed a significantly longer head line.

In another episode called "Health and Longevity," I used before-and-after prints of a young woman who was dying from a heroin addiction. When she first came to see Ghanshyam, she had a disturbingly short life line. In their sessions, he helped her find a purpose and a reason to live. Six months later, she had quit drugs and was working toward a teaching degree—and her life line was much longer!

Être bien dans sa peau was an instant success. By the end of the first episode the phones at the Center were ringing nonstop with people booking sessions and wanting to learn about palmistry. When the series wrapped, we had a 10-month waiting list for appointments.

We built upon the success of *Être bien dans sa peau* with two more shows: *Self-Discovery* and *À la portée de votre main* (Within Reach of Your Hand).

Self-Discovery was our first English show, which Kathy hosted. She invited most of the Center's staff to appear as guests—Ghanshyam and his daughter, Rekha, covered Vedic palmistry, Peter explained astrology; I described the healing properties of gems; Johanne talked about the importance of a balanced hand; and Denise received an on-air Ayurvedic massage. Everybody was involved, and Kathy was so natural on camera that the show was picked up and broadcasted across the entire country. When

Rekha moved out West, she was shocked to see herself on TV when she stopped to pick up milk at a convenience store!

Feedback was so positive that we were asked to shoot *À la portée de votre main* in front of a live audience, with a call-in line and guests who had unique professions, talents and challenges. The show tackled current social issues through the prism of palmistry. I shared the guests' handprints with the audience, who were then allowed to ask questions about the prints and the guests. Our "Women in Love" episode was a favorite among viewers. It had a guest panel that included a single working woman, a woman who abandoned her career for her man, a nun and a gay woman. Each woman's choices and convictions were reflected in their prints—choices they discussed and debated with the audience. The show gave us a way to demonstrate that palmistry could be used effectively in a public forum to educate and bring people together.

Every time we produced a new series, our client list grew—a sure sign that we were having an impact and getting our message across. After a few years doing cable shows, I was invited to be on *Claire Lamarche*, which, in Quebec, was the equivalent of appearing on *Oprah*. It was a live show with a massive viewership and large studio audience. The producers wanted me to read the handprints of celebrities hidden behind an onstage screen.

Everyone at the Center was thrilled! Some of the staff came to sit in the audience, while others worked backstage taking the celebrity's handprints. One staff member was assigned to pop singer Mitsou. As he was inking the beautiful, young singer's palms, she suffered a wardrobe malfunction and her tight black top popped open. Both Mitsou and our staff member stood frozen, aghast and unable to fix the situation as both their hands were covered in black ink! They had to summon help and, fortunately, Mitsou laughed and was a good sport about it—I read her hands several times over the coming years.

I definitely had some preshow jitters, but they disappeared after reading the prints of singer Judy Richard. Judy is a star in her own right, but she happened to be—and still is—married to Yvon Deschamps, one of the most famous comedic writer-performers in Quebec history.

While the audience could see Judy, I could not since she sat behind the screen a few feet away. The first thing I noticed when I looked at her handprints was an incredibly pronounced line of union, also known as the marriage line.

"Well," I said, "I can tell you from this handprint that behind a great man is a really great woman!" Judy burst out laughing behind the screen and so did the audience.

After Judy, I was handed the handprints of actor Marc-André Coallier, who was also hidden behind the screen. I saw his line of destiny coming from the base of his hand very close to the lifeline and said, "Your family can have a great influence on your career." Once again, the audience burst out laughing—everyone knew he had entered show business following in the footsteps of his father, actor-broadcaster Jean-Pierre Coallier.

All that laughter threw me off a bit, but when I looked out into the audience and saw Kathy sitting in the front row laughing along with everybody else, I knew I was on the right track and doing just fine.

After the show, the celebrity guests told me how impressed they were with their readings, and the next day, while driving to our Toronto office, we heard a radio commentator critiquing the previous night's *Lamarche* show.

"Frankly," he said, "if I were going to see a palmist, I would definitely go see Guylaine Vallée. She's the real deal."

Wow! I was speechless. By the next day, I was booked up with appointments for most of the year.

The *Claire Lamarche* show put palmistry and the Center in the spotlight. Interviews with print journalists and appearances on television and radio became a regular part of my practice—each one another opportunity to bring palmistry to the public.

But we also had opportunities to step out of the spotlight and bring palmistry to those considered to be a public danger.

The Happy Palmist

In the mid-90s a social service agency invited us to read the prints of inmates at two of Quebec's most notorious prisons—the Archambault Institution for men and the Tanguay detention center for women.

We were nervous at first. There had been a riot at Archambault a few years earlier and several guards had been brutally murdered. But we had been drawn to palmistry to help people—and who could benefit more by learning about their lines than prisoners? Perhaps their hands could show them why they had ended up behind bars and suggest ways to improve their lives.

We did a *Hora* for the time and day of our first prison visit. (A *Hora*, which is Sanskrit for "hour," is an astrological snapshot of a certain time and place.) According to the chart, we would arrive at Archambault when many of the planets were in the 6th house—the house of resistance, enemies, conflicts and imprisonment. What a coincidence!

When Kathy, Peter and I checked our bag of our inkpads and rollers through security and entered the common area where the inmates were waiting, we realized our fears had been unfounded. Most were covered in tattoos but they were as friendly as could be—greeting us with cookies and cakes.

The first prisoner who approached me was a young man in his early 20s who looked so sweet and innocent I could not imagine him hurting a fly. But when we walked to a more private area to do his reading I noticed two nervous-looking guards shadowing his every move. I figured he might not be as sweet as he looked, and definitely not innocent.

"Hi, I'm Guylaine," I said, reading his prints. We had been cautioned not to ask what their crimes were, so instead I asked, "Would you mind telling me how long you are in for?"

"I'm here for life," he said. "They say I raped and murdered someone."

A cold trickle of sweat ran down my back. I took a deep breath and asked, "Oh … Do you feel any remorse?"

"I was brought up in a tough neighborhood and I was expected to be a tough guy," he explained quickly. He was more eager to hear what his palms had to say than talking about himself.

The most noticeable thing about his hand was his huge Mars—which can (and in his case did) reflect an aggressive and volatile nature of a person who is compulsively self-serving, stubborn, short-tempered, possessive and prone to overreaction.

He also had short fingers—which aggravated his impulsive behavior, pushing him to act rashly with little concern about consequences; and he had a short thumb, revealing he was focused on daily survival and not looking toward the future.

"Does any of that make sense to you?" I asked, explaining in detail all that his hand had told me.

"Yeah … All of it does, I guess."

I told him he needed to find an appropriate, constructive outlet for his energy, perhaps by enrolling in a study program. And I suggested that he associate with inmates who were working toward early release through good behavior, who would be more positive and supportive.

He nodded in agreement.

"And you should try to plan for the future—even if you're in here for life, you're still young—find something you're passionate about and set a goal."

I showed him a couple of breathing exercises he could use to calm himself down and suggested he count to 10 whenever he felt his impulsive temper kicking in.

He promised to think about what we had talked about, thanked me and said he hoped he would see me again for another reading.

The next inmate I read was in his 70s. He was wearing expensive-looking slippers and had the smile and confidence of a lord of the manor presiding over his vassals. When he sat down, I discovered the reason he appeared so relaxed and happy—he was being released in a few days for good behavior. When I asked how much time he had served, he said, "I just finished 20 years for bank robbery."

Then he leaned toward me and confided in a low whisper, "I am looking forward to getting out and spending all my hard-earned cash." That was not all he was looking forward to. He said he had met a pretty young woman in the visitors' area and that they had stayed in contact. She had promised to be waiting for him when he got out.

He had a long Saturn finger, which in itself could suggest wisdom, reflection, discernment, patience and discipline. But he also had a very short head line, which deprived him of long-term vision and had short-circuited those great Saturn qualities. So, instead of relying on sober planning and hard work to achieve his goals, he took the path of least resistance, using his impressive reasoning abilities to plot get-rich-quick schemes, like robbing banks. He was not interested about his character traits, but was very interested about his young girlfriend on the outside. He wanted to know if she would actually be there waiting when he got out, and if she really was in love with an old man like him, or did she just want his money?

The more he thought about his girlfriend, the more uncertain he became about himself. His long Saturn—without the stabilizing influence of a long head line to channel his thoughts positively—had set his mental wheels in motion, and they were spinning with doubt and worry. I suggested some things he could do to overcome his insecurity. After the reading, he shuffled off pensively in his fancy slippers, reflecting on all we had discussed.

The last prisoner I saw had a beautiful palm with a deep love-of-truth line.

"What are you doing in prison?" I asked. "With this line, you could be a philosopher or college professor."

"I am doing life for murder," he said. "I was in the wrong place at the wrong time."

His love-of-truth line was well earned, though. He had become a Buddhist while in jail and, to help other inmates expand their horizons, had volunteered to be the prison librarian. He wanted to talk about his spiritual quest and walked with us as we were leaving; he would have walked us right out of the prison if a guard had not stopped him at the gate.

The inmates I met at Archambault were among the most receptive clients I have ever had, and I left feeling that we had done some good. But the Tanguay prison was a different story. There were no cakes or cookies. We were escorted into a large, empty room to wait for the female inmates. A loud bell started ringing, a metal door swung open and they came rushing toward us, pushing and shoving each other out of the way to be the first in line for a reading.

It was an oppressive atmosphere that vibrated with a constant threat of violence. The women were definitely not happy being there and were in constant competition with each other to prove who was the toughest in order to survive in that repressive environment. It was a tense and uncomfortable situation, but they were hungry to hear what we had to tell them. Unfortunately, most just wanted predictions—predictions that were not particularly pleasant.

"Will I get even? Will I get revenge on the man who got me locked up in here?" was one of the first questions I was asked.

When I asked the woman what she had done, she said, "Believe me, you don't want to know."

If they allowed me to, I described the negative influences in their palms, highlighted their positive signs and suggested things they could do to improve their situation and break the cycle they were trapped in. But their lives were so uncertain that they were not interested in long-term planning or preventative palmistry.

My final client was frail, timid and utterly terrified.

"I don't belong in this place—I'm so scared. They sent me here for not paying my taxes. I just have six months to serve, but I don't think I will survive that long."

Her entire hand was riddled with crisscrossing and conflicting lines, and her palm was beet-red—a sign of deep anxiety, which was understandable given her circumstances. She was filled with regret and saw no way to turn her life around.

She was very receptive to meditation, though, and I gave her a mantra to recite and a relaxing breathing technique to center her energy and help her envision a happier, more peaceful future. What she needed most was some hope and courage and, in the limited time we had together, I tried my best to give her some.

Being there made me think about Karma, and how our negative thoughts and actions can echo across time and lead us to such horrid places. It was not an enjoyable experience, but it was a valuable lesson in the education of a young palmist learning her art.

We returned to the Center with a collection of handprints to add to the criminal section of our gallery. I did not know it at the time, but we were about to set off on a pilgrimage that would lead us to the hands of a saint.

My parents in 1943, a year before they were married.

Dancing to the music of my brother's guitar when I was five years old.

With my cousin Gilles, working at an engagement party for one of my many relatives.

Me as a happy 12 year old.

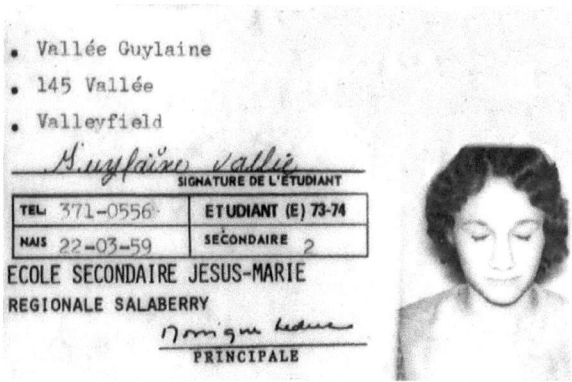

The disastrous haircut that led to my loss of
self-confidence in my teens.

The entire family. Top row, left to right: Caroline (Réjean's
daughter), Mimi, Normand, Denise (André's wife), Francine
(Réjean's wife), Monique (Gaston's wife), Guylaine and
Pierre (Gaston's son); middle row: Marcel, André, Mom,
Dad, Réjean, Gaston, Dominique (Gaston's daughter);
front row: Martin (André's son), Danny (Mimi's son) and
Charles (Gaston's second son). Not pictured is Jessica, Mimi's
daughter, who was not yet born.

Performing in the theater at Cégep de Jonquière at age 19.

Playing the role of singer Michèle Richard while in Jonquière.

Performance of *Sur le matelas* (On the Mattress) in Jonquière.

Returning from Paris in 1983.

Volunteering at my first street fair with Ghanshyam outside the Palmistry Center in Westmount.

My first *Autobiography of a Yogi*.

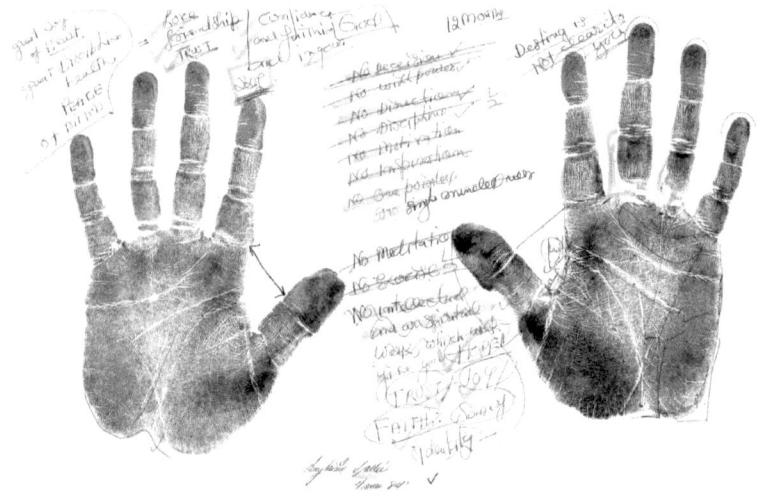

My first set of handprints with Ghanshyam's handwritten list of what I needed to improve.

Mounts
☽ Luna: Perception
♀ Venus: Love
♂- Mars negative: Physical Stamina
♂- Mars positive: Mental Endurance
♃ Jupiter: Purpose
♄ Saturn: Coordination
☉ Sun: Magnetism
☿ Mercury: Communication
☊ Rahu: Present Environment
☋ Ketu: Past, Karmic Debts

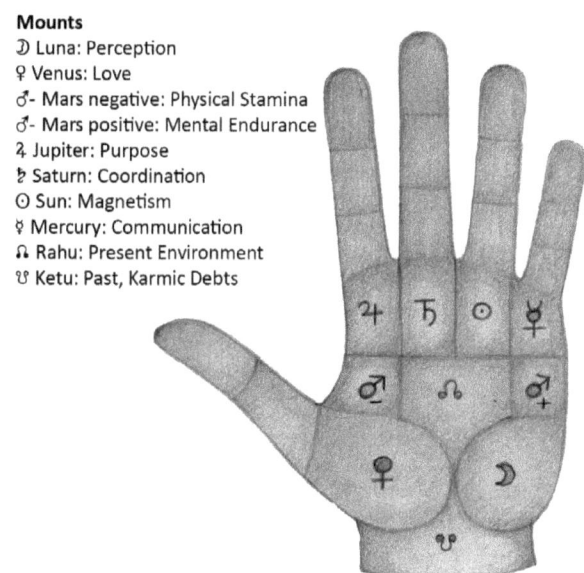

Mounts: The 10 mounts of the palm.

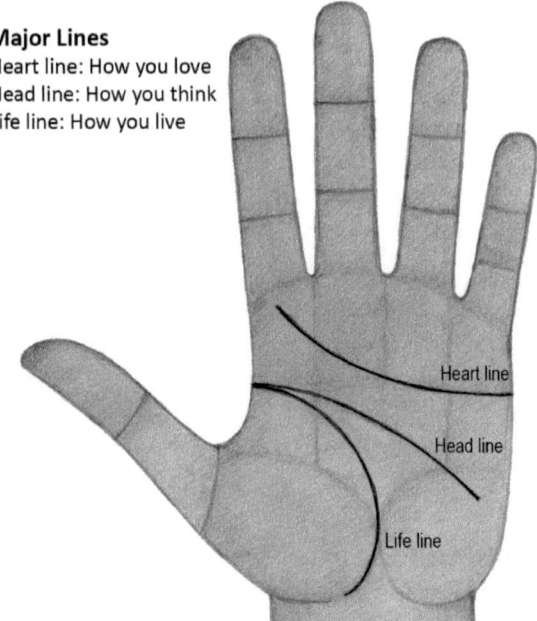

Major lines: The three major lines—heart, head and life.

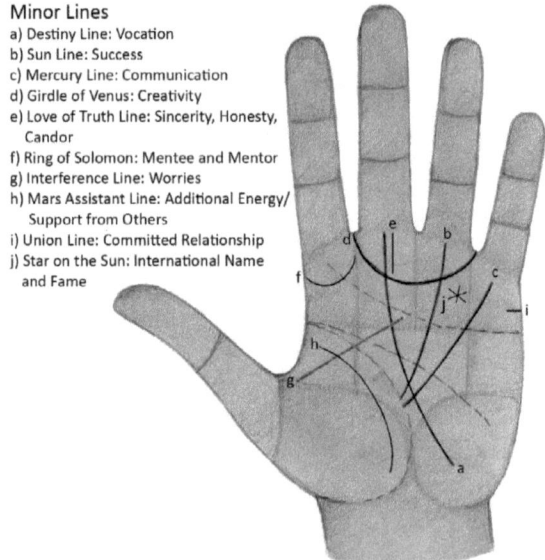

Minor lines: The minor lines, relating to our conscious level of awareness.

Happy to be back at the Palmistry Center after a six-month leave to write a script for submission in a contest.

Receiving support from Ghanshyam before a television appearance.

Reading Mitsou's palms.

Reading Lise Watier's hands after appearing on her television show *Évasion Beauté*.

Claire Lamarche congratulating me after a successful appearance on her wildly popular live show.

On the air at *Touche-à-tout*, a live radio program with Marguerite Blais.

With Juliette Powell on her show at *MuchMusic*.

With André Robitaille and Marina Orsini on *Tout l'monde debout*, a live radio program on Rouge fm.

With singer Ricky Martin at his home in Miami.

With Kathy and Peter, taking Ghanshyam's temperature after he fell ill in Calcutta.

Meeting Mother Teresa in her Calcutta mission with Kathy, Heather and Peter.

In Calcutta, meditating with Ghanshyam and Kathy in the attic room of Paramahansa's childhood home, where he had a vision of Mother Divine.

Afloat on the sacred Ganges River near Varanasi with Kathy and the gang saying a prayer for our ancestors.

Meeting with the Bhrigu in the remote Indian village of Karauli. Left to right: me, Denise, Kathy, Bhrigu and Ghanshyam.

Finding the Wellness Retreat Center, first shown to Ghanshyam by Lord Vishnu in a dream.

Kathy's burned-out office after a fire nearly destroyed the Palmistry Center. Amid the ruins, the picture of Paramahansa can be seen still intact.

Ghanshyam examining the aftermath of the fire at the Victoria Street Center one day after his birthday.

My therapy! After the fire, taking comfort in restoring old furniture for the guest rooms at the Wellness Center in Chénéville.

The Palmistry Center staff visiting Florida. Back row, left to right: me, Francis, Rémi, Peter, Ghanshyam and Jeannette; front row: Heather, Johanne, Jaysri, Denise, Grace, Sylvie and Kathy.

Me taking Wayne Dyer's prints in 1993 at the Silva Convention in Miami, where both Wayne and Ghanshyam were speakers.

Me with Gaston, Mimi and Réjean,
more united than ever.

One of the last pictures of
Mom with Mimi and me.

My follow-up handprints with lots of changes.

One of our palmistry classes with Ghanshyam.

CHAPTER 13

The Hands of a Saint

AFTER LEARNING HOW PROFOUNDLY Vedic palmistry and astrology could improve their lives, many of my clients said they wanted to travel to India to find inspiration and study the Vedic sciences. I would just shake my head and say, "What on earth for? Ghanshyam has brought India here for you!"

As long as I could learn from Ghanshyam at the Center and practice my Kriya Yoga at home, I saw no reason to make a pilgrimage to India seeking enlightenment—I could do that in Montreal!

There was a pilgrimage I *did* want to make. After reading *Autobiography of a Yogi*, I had a great desire to visit the Lake Shrine, the secluded spiritual retreat Paramahansa created atop Mount Washington, near the Self-Realization Fellowship headquarters in Los Angeles. Thousands of Kriya Yoga devotees visit that little piece of paradise each year during the SRF annual World Convocation; one summer, Kathy, Peter and I were among them.

The Lake Shrine is an Eden a few miles from the center of L.A., but a world away from the city's bustle and smog. It is nestled among 10 acres of woodland overlooking the Pacific Ocean, on the edge of a placid lake, ringed by low mountains and surrounded by exotic gardens designed to enhance meditation and self-reflection.

The shrine itself, a blend of eastern and western architecture crafted by Paramahansa, is intended to honor all major world religions and promote peace and communion with God. A portion of Mahatma Gandhi's ashes rest in a stone memorial not far from one of the Lake Shrine's greatest attractions—the "spiritual wishing well," where Paramahansa left both his footprints and handprints in fresh cement during a 1934 dedication ceremony.

Before we left for California, we asked Ghanshyam if he would like us to pick him up a souvenir from the SRF gift shop, and his request seemed simple enough.

"Kathy, the only thing I ask of you is to touch the handprints of Paramahansa on my behalf. That is my only wish!"

We spent several days at the convocation in central Los Angeles, reenergizing with hours of private and group meditation, and then joined a guided tour of the grounds and gardens of the Lake Shrine, intending to fulfill Ghanshyam's request. But, when we arrived at the wishing well, our tour guide, a saffron-robed SRF nun, announced sternly:

"You will notice a protective fence has been built around the wishing well to preserve our guru's handprints. Millions of hands have touched the prints and they have begun to erode. We must protect them, so kindly remember that touching is *not* allowed. No exceptions!"

From her manner we knew it was useless to plead with her. It was a dilemma, especially for Kathy, to whom Ghanshyam had specifically made his request. I wondered if he was deliberately challenging her to test her limits, something he frequently did with all of us. Kathy was guided by a strong Jupiter, which made decorum, propriety and family dignity enormously important to her. She was compelled to follow rules and regulations.

We stood with the rest of the crowd looking down at Paramahansa's handprints. They were beautiful, and even though it was frustrating not to be able to clearly make out his lines, we had his natal chart at the Center. His footprints marked the spot he stood more than half a century earlier as he was carrying out his mission to bridge the spiritual divide between the East and West and bring Kriya Yoga to the world. Beside his handprints was a message he had written in stone to inspire pilgrims for generations to come:

For Self-Realization I offer my hands, feet, and soul, and I pray all may do the same. Meditate and make the wish: 'May Thy love shine forever on the sanctuary of my devotion, and may I be able to awaken Thy love in all hearts.' Awake! Sleep no more.

"Paramahansa will understand," Kathy whispered, and she suddenly dropped to the ground in front of the entire busload of pilgrims and shot her arm out beneath the fence, laying her outstretched hand upon Paramahansa's palm prints.

There was a sudden flash of saffron as our disapproving tour guide–nun rushed toward us. Kathy got up and we quickly moved toward the bus, but were intercepted by a blue-uniformed SRF volunteer who skewered us with a look of disdain.

"How dare you be so disrespectful," she scolded Kathy, and continued reprimanding her for several minutes. Kathy shrugged her shoulders and said, "I had to do it. I wish I could tell you the whole story."

I was proud of her—my teaching idol was a rebel with a cause and had pushed herself beyond her boundaries.

The incident at the wishing well was the only wrinkle in an otherwise perfect trip, and we returned to the Center feeling revitalized and happy. Ghanshyam welcomed each of us home with one of his trademark bear hugs. And, with a mischievous smile on his lips and a twinkle in his eyes, he asked, "So, tell me! How was your trip?" We did not need to answer—he already knew.

In October 1995, Ghanshyam made a surprise announcement about a pilgrimage that would affect all of us.

"I am receiving an award in India. I am going for six weeks, and I want you all to come with me!"

The Indian Board of Alternative Medicines in Calcutta—the largest association of holistic and Ayurvedic healers in the world, with more than 80,000 practitioners—was honoring Ghanshyam with the Charak Memorial Award for his service to mankind through his "innovative work in preventative astro-palmistry, improving the mental and physical health of thousands of people, and restoring balance and harmony to interpersonal relationships."

We were thrilled that Ghanshyam was getting the recognition he so rightly deserved—and were stunned by his invitation to join him in India. No one knew what to say, except thank you, and that we were too broke to afford such an expensive trip.

"Don't worry, the money will come if we are positive and meditate and pray with good intentions."

And, lo and behold, the money did come. Somehow we all found a way to finance the trip.

It looked as though I was going to be an accidental pilgrim, which was just fine with me. While I had never planned on going to India, I welcomed the opportunity to visit the homeland of my two greatest teachers—Ghanshyam and Paramahansa. And I would have plenty of company—including Ghanshyam's wife, Chanchala, and their eldest son, Keero, there would be 15 in our expedition.

We were all concerned that, with no one left in the office, we would have to close the Center for the first time in its 22-year history. But, once again, someone up there was watching over us and sent an angel to help—she arrived in the form of Jacinthe Côté, one of our newest students.

Jaysri, as Ghanshyam had nicknamed her, had recently visited the Holy Land, where she had had a spiritual awakening while praying in a cave in the same Judean desert where Jesus had retreated to for 40 days before beginning his ministry. When she returned to Montreal, she had a consultation with Ghanshyam and immediately enrolled in our Diploma Program. When Jaysri saw our reluctance to leave the Center unattended, she said, "Go have a wonderful trip! I'll be here every day to take care of things."

It was a great relief knowing we were leaving the Center in her capable and caring hands. There would be no consultations during our two-month absence, but our clients and students were as happy as we were for Ghanshyam to get his due.

Three days after Christmas 1995, our troupe from the Center left the frigid streets of Montreal behind, only to be halted by custom officials suspicious of Ghanshyam's bulging and extraordinarily heavy luggage. We were pretty curious about them ourselves, but he was tight-lipped about what he was transporting. We boarded our plane just in time, and after an exhausting 24-hour flight—during which Ghanshyam, who was terrified of flying, meditated continuously—we touched down in Calcutta, bleary-eyed and disorientated.

What a culture shock! Even in the middle of the night, the airport was pandemonium: dozens of porters grabbed our belongings and headed off in all directions. Luckily Chanchala, who spoke Hindi, was standing there and was able to corral our belongings. The heat, dust, noise and poverty of Calcutta assailed us when we stepped out of the airport. Cows wandered in the middle of the streets, dozens of beggars surrounded us and we were shocked to see lepers sleeping on the road.

We stayed at the Fairlawn Hotel in the center of Calcutta, where we were greeted by the proprietress, Violet Smith, an eccentric grand dame who carried a little white poodle tucked under her arm. Violet wore flamboyant outfits and heavy makeup and possessed an aura of having seen it all—as did the 200-year-old hotel she had inherited from her mother. The tranquil green courtyard of the Fairlawn, fringed with potted palm trees, was a welcome refuge from the dust and chaos of the streets. The constant caws of high, circling crows drowned out the traffic and further added to the mystique. Violet told us about the celebrities she had hosted over the years, and that she and her hotel had been featured in the movie *City of Joy,* starring Patrick Swayze, who played a young American doctor working in Calcutta's poorest slum.

We saw the slum ourselves. And while I was overwhelmed by the extreme poverty, I was also deeply moved by the dignity and calmness in the eyes of so many of Calcutta's most destitute residents. Hundreds of families lived, ate and slept in the streets, yet the women's saris were spotlessly clean and, despite their desperate situation, they smiled and laughed as they cared for their children. I was humbled by their resilience and learned that even in squalor the human spirit can touch God and find joy within.

We had several days before the conference started, which allowed us time to visit Paramahansa's boyhood home. We meditated in the sky-blue attic room, where he had once experienced a vision of Mother Divine (the Virgin Mary in Catholic ideology) after his own mother had died. We also sat in his bedroom, where he said he "discovered God." As we walked the dusty streets by Paramahansa's house, we felt we had stepped back in time and were retracing his footsteps, although we had to contend with much more air and noise pollution. There were few cars and only a million people living in Calcutta when he was a boy; now there were millions of cars and 12 million people. We wore scarves over our faces to filter the dust and smog and cover our ears to drown out the blasting of car horns.

The air quality was so bad that Kathy and I developed ugly rattles deep in our chest. Dr. Khrisen Kumar Kapoor, a real gentleman who was assigned to us by the Board of Alternative Medicine to be our guide in Calcutta, took us to his wife's clinic, where she performed acupressure on our hands, which cured us of our aliment.

As we left the clinic, we saw some kids flying kites from the roof, then Kathy noticed the street sign—Park Lane. "I can't believe it!" she said, excitedly. "This is the street my dad played on as boy—he told us about running up and down this very spot and flying kites on the roof!" Kathy's great-grandfather had come to India from Ireland to escape the potato famine and opened a chemist's shop in Northern India. Her father, who grew up in India, had shared many of his childhood memories with Kathy and Peter. We were amazed by the synchronicity of our clinic visit, and I had that old feeling someone was watching over us.

We were not the only ones to get sick in Calcutta. A day before the conference began, Ghanshyam fell seriously ill with malaria, developing a high fever and slipping into a coma. We were unfamiliar with the hospital system in the country and were incredibly worried. When Ghanshyam missed his keynote address at the conference, Dr. Kapoor dropped by to check on him and inserted so many acupuncture needles up and down Ghanshyam's body that he looked like a porcupine. Peter and I sat with him throughout the night until the needles were removed in the morning, then we all took turns watching over him. Kathy was alone with Ghanshyam on the third day of his coma, when he suddenly bolted up in bed and looked at her with urgent intensity.

"Kathy, please, you must go see Mother Teresa! Make sure to get her handprints!" Then he fell back onto the bed, lapsing into unconsciousness.

Kathy rushed to the payphone across the street and somehow found the number of Mother Teresa's Missionaries of Charities.

"Hello. May I speak to Mother Teresa?"

"Acha! Acha!"

Kathy was shocked to realize she was speaking with Mother Teresa.

"I need to see you," Kathy blurted out.

"Come now!"

Kathy ran back to the hotel and gathered everyone she could find—Peter, me and our companion, Heather. We grabbed our camera and printing gear, jumped into a cab and headed into one of the world's poorest neighborhoods. Mother Teresa's mission was a haven amid the surrounding filth and hovels, where the dedicated nuns of her Order cared for the impoverished and the sick, especially those suffering from leprosy, who were most shunned by society.

We were surprised to find a lot of other people lined up to see her and we sat by a curtained partition to wait with everyone else. Suddenly, the curtain parted and there she was, Mother Teresa.

I bowed down and touched her feet, a sign of respect in India. She was barefoot; I noticed her feet were unusually wide and I was struck by how gnarled and deformed they were. They were beautiful, like the roots of an ancient and mighty tree that no storm could topple. Yet, when I stood up and looked at her, she radiated a lightness that was as ethereal as a spirit.

She took Kathy by the arm and gave her a handful of medals bearing the image of the Virgin Mary.

"Come and help me distribute these."

We all followed behind—awestruck—as Mother Teresa and Kathy passed out the medals to those who had been waiting to see her, all the while trying to find the right moment to take her handprints—without success. She was constantly on the move and waved off our requests to examine her palms. But I guess she sensed how important it was to us and finally stopped and turned to us.

"What is it you want to see in these old hands?"

She held her hands out toward us with her palms facing up.

My God, what beautiful hands!

She had an exceptionally long heart line in both her palms, each with three branches, revealing her deep love and compassion for humanity and a tremendous spiritual insight. Each branch was of equal size, a sign that her loving deeds touched the hearts of people around the world.

Her destiny line stretched from the Mount of Moon at the base of her hand all the way up to her Saturn finger, showing her deep empathy and power to act as a force of good and inspiration to others.

She also possessed an incredible truth line, representing her unshakable love of God. Her intense head line, running straight across her hand to her Mars positive, expressed her unwavering perseverance and dedication to her cause. And it was no surprise to us that her hands were emblazoned with many marks of wisdom.

Even though we were not able to take her handprints, the image of those magnificent palms was forever engraved in my memory.

She smiled and we felt a wave of love, devotion and serenity wash over us. There was no ego in her, only Divine presence. We were honored to be in the company of one of God's angels on Earth, a living saint truly dedicated to the service of humanity.

Signs prohibiting photography were posted everywhere, yet she was gracious enough to pose with us for several pictures. We kissed her on the cheek, touched her feet and left with joyous and humbled hearts.

When we returned to the hotel we were shocked and greatly relieved to find Ghanshyam—who was in a coma only hours earlier—sitting upright in bed eating a big bowl of dhal. His fever was gone and he had a big smile on his face. He did not remember anything about asking Kathy to go see Mother Teresa, but he was overjoyed that we had. It was a miraculous day!

For the rest of the week, we attended the conference and learned about new and innovative methods of Ayurvedic healing, and we were all on hand with several hundred other participants from around the world when Ghanshyam received his award. When the applause died down, the presenter called out Kathy's name. It was a big surprise to everyone. Kathy was not sure what to do until Ghanshyam, with a devilish grin on his face, beckoned her to the podium, where she was awarded with a Ph.D. for her years of work in astro-palmistry. And then, one by one, the rest of us were summoned to the front and presented with bachelor's degrees—and each of us was also awarded a special diploma allowing us to practice astro-palmistry anywhere in India.

Suddenly, Ghanshyam's mysteriously heavy suitcases made sense. He had sent our credentials to the Board weeks before we left Canada and had our diplomas prepared in Montreal—beautiful gold-plated plaques mounted on pieces of solid oak with our names and degrees engraved in the precious metal. Each one weighed four or five pounds and he had lugged them all halfway around the world to surprise us and ensure that we shared in his special moment.

My eyes teared up as gratitude and appreciation flooded my heart. I remembered Ghanshyam saying years before, when I left the Center to enter that screenwriting contest, "If you win, I win."

And now I understood that when Ghanshyam won, we all won.

CHAPTER 14

Into the Heart of India

WE LEFT CALCUTTA WITH our diplomas in hand and a great sense of pride, traveling to the outskirts of the city to the SRF ashram at Dakshineswar for two days of peace and quiet. Paramahansa founded the ashram in the mid-1930s to promote the practice of Kriya Yoga in India. It is a stately and beautiful retreat, which, aside from the hordes of nighttime mosquitoes that drove me beneath the shelter of a giant net, was a restful respite from downtown Calcutta.

We did our morning energization exercise alongside the monks while looking out over the Ganges River, then borrowed bicycles and rode to the nearby Kali Temple—Kali is another manifestation of Mother Divine. Paramahansa brought his brother-in-law to the Kali Temple to put him on the path of spiritual enlightenment after his sister complained to him about her husband's narrow-minded outlook. The visit worked—Paramahansa's brother-in-law reformed and began practicing Kriya Yoga! While the brother-in-law waited outside the temple, Paramahansa meditated inside, where he had a vision of Mother Kali, as had Ramakrishna, the 19th-century mystic whom Paramahansa greatly admired.

Mother Divine appeared to Ramakrishna as an ocean of light, to which all humans have access, and, like Paramahansa, he preached the universality of religions. "Many are the names of God, and infinite the forms that lead us to know Him," he once said. "In whatsoever name or form you desire to call Him, in that very form and name you will see Him."

Adjacent to the Kali Temple is the enormous Ramakrishna Temple, where Ramakrishna shared his life with his wife and spiritual counterpart, Sarada Devi. We meditated in their private room at the foot of their enormous bed until it was time to return to Paramahansa's ashram and catch our bus to Howrah Railway Station to begin the second leg of our pilgrimage.

I had read a lot about miracles happening in India, but once I was actually there I realized what a miracle it was just getting somewhere on time in the wonderfully chaotic country! I also realized what an onerous task Peter had been assigned: as group leader he was responsible for coordinating travel plans, ensuring the 15 of us (and our 30 pieces of luggage) did not get lost or separated, that we had clean water and that we made each and every one of our countless connections—one missed train or bus could derail the entire trip, which almost happened at the very outset.

The bus to Howrah Station never arrived at the ashram—3 million people were pouring into the city that day for a major political rally and there was more bedlam in the streets than the normal level of insanity. The monks finally located a broken-down relic for us that once functioned as a school bus and, after 30 minutes of praying, meditating, cussing and coaxing, the engine sputtered to life and we lurched and backfired though the protesters to the train station.

Howrah Station is the oldest railway terminal in India; it resembles a medieval fortress but functions more like an asylum. It is a city onto itself with tens of thousands of people crammed into the cavernous space that amplifies and echoes the deafening roar of that seething mass of humanity. Scores of families camped out on the platform, squatting around cooking fires, washing their clothes and breast-feeding their children amid the crush of daily commuters. A pack of fraudulent porters snatched our bags, disappearing with our suitcases on top of their heads. Peter and Keero chased them down and then pushed, pulled and prodded us into our car. A few minutes later a whistle blew, and great clouds of steam belched from the smoke stack of our old locomotive, shrouding the platform in a hazy fog as the heavy metal wheels beneath us began to groan. We were on our way.

Our train was a microcosm of Indian society, with plush, finely upholstered private compartments for the privileged at one end and hard wooden benches for peasants, goats and chickens at the other. We were in the middle, with small sitting compartments featuring a double row of fold-down sleeping berths above the seats. Those passenger cars were our home away from home for the next month and I grew to love traveling across the vast subcontinent by train—even though it was a bit scary at times. Despite heavy metal doors and two guards posted in each car, a band of dacoits (thieves) slipped into the train and a wedding party in the neighboring compartment lost all their money and gifts.

In the city of Allahabad, we were caught in a riot during a mini Kumbh Mela, a 2,500-year-old religious festival attracting tens of millions of bathers to the flood plains of the Yamuna and Ganges Rivers. It is the largest and most peaceful religious gathering in the world, but that night hundreds of young hooligans swarmed our train. Luckily, the guards saw what was coming and yanked us on board just in time, managing to fight the mob off and wrestle the doors shut. But as the train sat in the station, the crowd pounded on our compartment window with long bamboo poles until the glass splintered. It felt like an eternity before the train began to move. Had it not left when it did, I am certain the window would have shattered and the rioters would have climbed in on top of us.

At another stop, Ghanshyam and I hopped off to buy food at a rail side kiosk; we turned around with the meals in our hands to find the train pulling out of the station. We ran down the platform to catch it, passing the food to Kathy and Peter through an open window before leaping onto the steps of the moving locomotive. It was all part of the great adventure.

Our plan was to travel several thousand kilometers across India in a rough triangle, heading far north to see where Kathy and Peter's great-grandfather had lived in Mussoorie, then southwest to the fabled cities of Jaipur and Udaipur before flying home from New Delhi. But our first destination was the spiritual heart of India, the ancient city of Varanasi.

Varanasi sits on the western shore of the Ganges and has been continuously inhabited for 5,000 years, making it one of the oldest cities on Earth. It is such a holy site that many Hindus believe those who are cremated and have their ashes scattered in the Ganges at Varanasi achieve *moksha*—meaning, they are freed from the cycle of death and rebirth and their souls ascend directly to heaven. This is no small thing in Hinduism—who would choose to suffer through a hundred thousand lifetimes if it is possible to be reunited with God in a single moment? Consequently, "death hotels," or "liberation houses" accommodating the sick and dying do a brisk trade in Varanasi. And for those who can afford firewood, the funeral pyres, known as ghats, burn around the clock. The presence of death is a constant part of life in Varanasi and wherever we went we saw funeral processions carrying bodies toward the pyres. I almost joined one of those processions when I impatiently tried to squeeze by a lumbering oxcart in a narrow street and got my ribs slammed up against the ox's long horn. Fortunately, no serious damage was done and I was reminded of Ghanshyam's advice to slow down and be more patient—which India was teaching me to do.

We hired rickshaws one day and, as we bumped along the rutted road, I thought of the *Bhagavad Gita* passages describing Lord Krishna driving his chariot into battle during the great Kurukshetra War and his discussions about reincarnation with his companion, the famous archer Arjuna.

Krishna told Arjuna that the cycle of life and death can be ended only through enlightenment, when we have paid the Karmic debt we have accumulated through lifetimes of selfishness by living a totally selfless life, free of ego and in complete service to God. Krishna also said Kriya Yoga hastens our journey to enlightenment, and I was glad I practiced it daily—I did not expect to have my ashes scattered in the Ganges at Varanasi.

We had hoped to see the golden rays of the rising sun dance across the Ganges—a spectacle for which Varanasi is also famous, and hired a rowboat to take us onto the water. But the morning was overcast and sullen, casting everything in a colorless shade of gray—everything except the brilliantly red sari of a woman whose body had just been laid atop a ghat. We watched respectfully as the pyre was lit ablaze and she was consumed in orange flame, saying prayers that she actually did achieve *moksha* and her soul would speed heavenward. Then we lit candles for our own loved ones and set them afloat on the surface of the sacred Ganges. Denise's candle flipped over and sputtered out as soon as she placed it in the water. She looked at it drift away and then burst out laughing.

"That's my dad's sense of humor for you," Denise smiled. "He never took these things too seriously."

From Varanasi, we continued north to the foothills of the Himalayas to search for the home of Peter and Kathy's great-grandfather, the sailor who left Ireland in the 19th century and opened a pharmacy in one of the remotest parts of India. We traveled by train to Dehradun and then endured a long, harrowing bus ride along a narrow, winding, cloud-shrouded mountain road to Mussoorie. The ravine below was littered with the twisted wrecks of vehicles that had failed to successfully navigate the twisty pass and I clutched the seat in front of me the entire way expecting us to plunge to our deaths at every turn.

Mussoorie is known as a Hill Station, one of the high-elevation towns built by the British to escape the unbearable summer heat of the Indian plains and valleys. Mussoorie certainly fit the bill—we had to buy thick woolen hats and mitts from roadside vendors to stay warm and even wore them inside while eating hot soup to stop from trembling in the cold mountain air.

Peter asked around about his great-grandfather. No one recalled the Keogh family, but everyone remembered the pharmacy, which had been converted into a restaurant and that was still furnished with his ancestor's antiques. In a nearby store, Peter found the glass jars his great-grandfather used to mix healing compounds of spices and minerals. We could still smell the camphor in some of the fragile containers, which Peter and Kathy carefully wrapped to carry back to Canada as a gift for their dad.

Meanwhile, Ghanshyam had set off to explore the town, happening upon an abandoned Catholic Church buried behind a mound of overgrown brush. He pushed through a rusted, wrought iron gate and discovered a sprawling cemetery running up the entire side of the hill. We searched for the gravestone of Peter and Kathy's relative until the sun began setting. In desperation, Kathy exclaimed, "Ghanshyam, it's getting dark! We can't have come all this way not to find the grave!"

"Remember what Paramahansa said," Ghanshyam responded. "If you are having trouble reaching your goal, ask for Babaji's assistance and he will help you."

Ghanshyam sat down on a rock and immediately began to meditate. A moment later a member of the group shouted, "I found it! I found it!"

We gathered around the vine-covered, four-foot high Celtic cross marking Patrick Ambrose Keogh's grave and said a prayer for him. I looked beyond the cemetery at snow-capped peaks of the Himalayas. It suddenly occurred to me that Great-Grandfather Keogh had been living in this spot when Lahiri Mahasaya met Babaji on a Himalayan mountainside in 1861 and learned the secret of Kriya Yoga, a secret passed to Paramahansa, who then brought it to the West—where Ghanshyam discovered it and introduced it to me. Again, I was astonished by the synchronicity we found on our pilgrimage.

We set out from Mussoorie for the 1,000-kilometer journey to Udaipur, leaving the Himalayas and traveling by train across the wide deserts of Rajasthan, where I could see camels trekking across the red sand dunes. We stopped in Jaipur to take in the magnificent temples and other splendors of the famous "Pink City," and finally arrived in Udaipur to visit the famous Floating Palace in Lake Pichola.

While in Udaipur, Ghanshyam heard of an authentic Bhrigu astrologer in a remote village a three-hour drive north of the city. We were all tired and worn out, so not thrilled at the prospect of a long ride over rugged roads in an Indian taxi.

"This is a very rare opportunity that we can't afford to miss," Ghanshyam insisted, so off we went to consult with Bhrigu Nathulal Vyas in the dusty hamlet of Karauli.

In Hindu mythology, Bhrigu is the son of the god Brahma, who created the universe. It is said that thousands of years before the birth of Christ, Bhrigu used the movement of the planets and complex mathematical configurations to determine the destinies of all those who would ever be born. He wrote his findings down on a collection of palm leaves; the text became known as the *Bhrigu Samhita* (*Samhita* being Sanskrit for "collection"). The palm leaves were eventually preserved in more permanent forms of recordkeeping, but those records and the art of interpreting the *Bhrigu Samhita* itself, were largely lost to time. There were only a handful of Bhrigus still left in India, which was why Ghanshyam was so insistent we visit.

We pulled up to Nathulal's house just as an official ministerial government car was pulling away. It was hard to miss because, other than camels, there seemed to be no other mode of transportation in the village.

Nathulal was a bearded, wiry and extremely fit 50-year-old with an ancient face, intense dark eyes and a booming voice. He welcomed us into his home and we sat around him in a semicircle on the concrete floor of what appeared to be his office. After taking a cursory glance at our palms, he opened one of the many large green boxes that resembled old steamer trunks lining the walls of the room. He rifled through the countless files inside the box and retrieved the ones that apparently had corresponding file numbers for each of our destinies. He sat in the lotus position, warned us not to interrupt him with too many questions and then began our readings—which were mind-bogglingly accurate—as Ghanshyam translated.

"It is sanctioned that at this hour on this day in this year I am to read to you from the *Samhita*," Nathulal began. Years later, when he became famous for predicting the ascendency of a local politician to the presidency of India, we learned that the Bhrigu did not have the records in his files of *everyone* ever born—only those destined to visit him at a particular time. We also discovered that, in preparation for such intense readings, he spent eight hours each day practicing *sādhanā*, a deep and intensely spiritual form of meditation.

"Your parents are still living and you have two sisters and one brother, still living," he told Peter. He then added. "Your future wife is here with you." We all looked around at each other, wondering what exactly was contained in those mysterious files—Peter and Johanne had fallen in love shortly after she had started at the Center, but it was not at all obvious that they were together as we sat there. At the time, even they did not know they would be married. (But, sure enough, they tied the knot a few years after our India trip.)

At the start of Ghanshyam's reading, Nathulal confirmed that he was married with two sons and a daughter, and then said to him:

"Your main purpose in life is to help others. You have a deep love for God and seek to know God through meditation and devotion to your guru. Your destiny involves a foreign country, which is why you left India. You have a blessed, auspicious life. You have done great things. You do preventive work of *hast jyotish*—bringing the past and present together in a way to help improve people's futures. That is your main destiny—to promote that work. At your place of work you always are playing the Gayatri Mantra."

We looked at each other in amazement. Not only was he spot-on about Ghanshyam's devotion and work, just a couple of months before we left for India, Peter and Serge Fiori had recorded a musical version of the Gayatri Mantra and we played the tape at the Center around the clock.

Nathulal also predicated something for Ghanshyam that would become a huge part of our lives in the future. "You will establish a *hast jyotish*-related research institution and ashram, a school where people will come to study and stay and find food and shelter. There will be many buildings and a large property requiring much work. And there will be a statue of Mother Divine at this location—you are protected and supported and inspired to do great things there, by God's grace."

I was initially embarrassed with what he said when it was my turn.

"Your horoscope is unique among millions. You are on a definite path that is destined by God to show the light to other people. You have moved away from your birthplace to serve others. Your destiny is *hast jyotish*, Ayurvedic medicine and other forms of healing to help others. You have a deep longing to communicate with cosmic forces and will love God throughout your life and strive to bring that ideal love to all humanity."

It was very flattering and reassuring, but what he said next was so specific and accurate, it shocked me.

"Your mother is still living and your father has died. When he died, he held you in high status and in his heart recognized what you were doing. Of your many brothers, one has something wrong with his mind, it does not work properly. People may think he is a lunatic, but he is not. His emotional or mental health has been a source of much anxiety for you and caused you a great deal of pain. Your elder sister will have another companion—she is meant to love again. You yourself have the choice to marry, but you are already married to your calling—that dedication is your marriage. Destiny has chosen your friends and they are very helpful and supportive to you.

"You have no desire for money, but you are interested in acting and are a good actress; you will work in film or TV and reach many people. People will be amazed by your predictions."

He paused and said: "You should develop patience by developing household interests, like cooking—you do everything too fast, so it is not a good idea for you to own a car."

Everyone laughed at that prediction and sound advice. Nathulal had given us much to think about and had bolstered our faith in the science of *jyotish*. And much of what he said would come to pass in the coming years.

We left Karauli and traveled to New Delhi, where Ghanshyam would stay to visit family and we would board our flight back to Canada.

On our last day in India, most of the group decided to go to Agra to see the Taj Mahal, but Kathy and I decided to stay in New Delhi to go shopping. Ghanshyam, who was spending the day hunting for rare books on *hast jyotish*, stopped us before we left the hotel and said, "Today is the day you ride an elephant."

Elephants are revered in India as symbols of wisdom, and Ghanshyam, who had a special affinity for the elephant-headed God Ganesha, believed riding one was very auspicious.

"Sure, Ghanshyam, that sounds like a *great* idea," we snickered as we left to go shopping.

We were rummaging in a souvenir shop when I spotted a large statue of Hanuman, the half-human, half-monkey deity who is the central figure in the epic poem the Ramayana. Ghanshyam used to call me Hanuman when I first started working at the Center, which I took as a great compliment once I had read that amazing literary masterpiece.

Hanuman possesses the strength of several deities and is so fiercely loyal to Lord Rama that he battled the forces of evil to rescue Rama's wife, Sita, when she was abducted by a demon. In many paintings, Hanuman is seen holding his chest open to reveal the image of Rama and Sita tattooed upon his heart. That idea moved me because I often felt my loved ones were tattooed on my own heart. In Vedic astrology, Hanuman is associated with the planet Mars because he is a warrior and defender, the one who triumphs over evil, and I deeply admired the courage and devotion he represented.

I wanted to buy the Hanuman statue, but I could not afford it. The shopkeeper wanted an outrageous sum and while Kathy and I were trying to haggle down the price, a giant elephant appeared at the door.

The elephant's owner smiled in at us. "Would the ladies like a ride?"

We looked at each other in astonishment. Sometimes Ghanshyam was so intuitive it was unnerving. What else could we do? It was our day to ride an elephant!

Even with the owner's assistance, it was quite an ordeal to climb onto the bamboo platform strapped to the noble beast's back. By the time I scrambled on top and hoisted Kathy up alongside me, a small crowd had surrounded us, delighted to see two young Western women braving such an unusual situation. We were frighteningly high and precariously seated; the elephant had not taken more than a couple of steps when Kathy started screaming and yelled, "I'm outta here!" She jumped off the elephant's back and into the arms of the cheering onlookers. I made it a little further down the street before dismounting, only to see the shopkeeper running toward me waving the Hanuman statue over his head.

"Half price, half price! For the elephant lady, Hanuman is half price!"

Somehow Ghanshyam always knew what we needed to do.

I carried my Hanuman statue onto the plane with me for the homeward flight to Montreal. I would need his strength and courage in the coming years when disaster would test my resolve and scatter our happy band of pilgrims, who had built so many wonderful memories together in India.

CHAPTER 15

Dreams and Disaster

MY JOURNEY TO INDIA coincided with a subtle shift in the Cosmos, closing one chapter of my life while opening another.

Astrologically, the 10-year Moon *dasha* I had entered prior to joining the Center ended as I was packing my bags for India. By the time we touched down in Calcutta, I had moved into a seven-year Mars *dasha*. As I mentioned earlier, in Vedic astrology *dashas* are periods of time during which we are strongly influenced by the characteristics of a particular astral body. The significance of being in a Moon *dasha* during my first decade at the Center became increasingly clear as I delved deeper into astrology.

Moon is gentle, nurturing and highly creative, making a Moon *dasha* a fortuitous time to put down roots, build strong bonds of friendship and family, and develop oneself through study, dedication and devotion. When surrounded by a positive and loving atmosphere, it is an amazingly fertile period for personal, professional and spiritual growth. In my case, all those wonderful possibilities were amplified because my ascendant sign is Cancer, and Cancer is ruled by the Moon!

Mars, on the other hand, is the planet of energy, action and war—that is the reason Mars has been symbolized by the soldier or warrior since the time of the Ancient Greeks and Romans. A Mars *dasha* can be a powerful period for acquiring property and career development, but it can also be a period of hardship and struggle. As with any warrior, during a Mars *dasha*, we can come under attack—by enemies, by accidents and other forms of malefic energy. But a Mars *dasha* does not necessarily mean we are in a negative phase of our life, just a highly challenging one. Like a Moon *dasha*, it can be a great opportunity to grow, but growth during a Mars *dasha* is often measured against our response to negative situations—it is a battleground where our courage, strength and fortitude are tested. And I certainly would be tested over the coming seven years.

When I returned from India I headed directly to the Center, which I now truly considered to be my home. Passing through our Handprint Gallery, I admired the collection of familiar palms displayed along the walls. During the past decade, I had studied every one and printed many of them myself. The gallery filled me with a sense of achievement—I had traveled a great distance and accomplished so much since first arriving at the Center in search of a purpose. I had found my purpose and so much more. I was happy, and had grown personally, professionally and spiritually.

The Center was growing as well, and I took pride in my contribution to its development. In fact, we were growing so quickly it was hard to keep up. We had more clients than ever and our classes were overflowing. Word-of-mouth had spread about our Diploma Program and students were coming to us from across Canada, the U.S. and Europe. We needed to expand and find more space, a place that provided the healthiest environment possible for our clients and students to enhance the positive benefits of everything we had to offer. Our goal was to build a Wellness Center in a country setting with unlimited fresh air, sunshine and clean water, somewhere close enough to the city for an easy commute yet distant enough to escape the stress of urban living and commune with nature. We also needed a building that could accommodate large lectures, classrooms for yoga and meditation, and studios for the many holistic healing therapies we envisioned practicing. It was a harder task than we had imagined—we had been looking at property for several years throughout Quebec, Ontario, New York, New England and even

Florida, but nothing felt quite right. It was a permanent item on our to-do list, another addition to the ambitious schedule we had mapped out for the coming months.

I left the gallery and walked into my office, hanging my new bachelor's degree from India on the wall and placing my statue of Hanuman, my Mars warrior and courageous hero, on the little inspirational altar beside my desk. And then I got to work; there was much to do. Besides being booked for radio and television appearances and out-of-town readings, classes and lectures, we had just started working on Ghanshyam's first book, *Love in the Palm of Your Hand*. It was a major project that was, literally, a labor of love for everyone at the Center.

Many, if not most, of our clients originally came to us seeking help with their love lives, and not just looking to find Mr. or Mrs. Right, but sincerely searching for ways to fill their entire lives with love. They wanted to learn how to create more loving families and express their feelings in a more open and caring manner; to mend fractured relationships and keep waning love alive; to learn how to love themselves and accept love from others; and to understand how to experience the love of God. Ghanshyam had always believed that God, the source of all love, resides in the human heart; in many ways, his life's work was dedicated to that cause—to connecting people with their own hearts.

The intention of *Love in the Palm of Your Hand* was to show how palmistry can be practiced at home to create a loving foundation upon which to build one's life. It was a hugely important issue to us and we all pitched in to get the job done, as did many of our friends and families. I was responsible for sifting through thousands of our handprints to select real-life case histories to illustrate the book's central theme; Ghanshyam drew on the wealth of his 35 years as a practicing palmist; and Kathy and Peter worked tirelessly on the manuscript with the help of our friend Pat Conway, Head of the English department at Vanier College.

On top of all that, we had a backlog of clients Jaysri had booked while we were away exploring India. As promised, Jaysri held down the fort for us and even taught one of my large library classes so that I did not have to cancel it during my absence. She had never addressed an audience before and, even with a stack of our notes to follow, she was terrified to teach a subject she was still learning herself.

"When I saw all the people who'd come to listen, I began shaking," she told me. "But the moment I stepped up to the podium I became calm and confident and was even able to have fun. I could feel that you guys were praying for me."

We *had* been praying for her, and she picked up on that positive energy from 12,000 kilometers away. Jaysri received stellar reviews from her students that night but her true gift lay elsewhere—Ghanshyam had spotted it during her first consultation.

"You were born with the hands of a healer; healing is your passion and it's the passion you should pursue," Ghanshyam told her, and he offered her an opportunity to do just that.

Part of the plan for the Wellness Center was providing Ayurvedic massage, which is extremely helpful in lengthening the spine, freeing our natural breath, removing energy blockages and opening the chakras. Even though Jaysri had no professional massage experience, Ghanshyam was confident in her gift; he asked her if she would be interested in being the Center's first full-time massage therapist and, when she accepted, he sent her off to college for therapeutic massage and reflexology training. Meanwhile, we continued our hunt for a suitable site to fulfill our dream of building a Wellness Center, and we finally found it—in a dream!

In November 1997, Ghanshyam, Kathy, Peter and I attended a seminar in Niagara Falls on Magnet Therapy, a healing technique we intended to include at our new facility. On our way home to Montreal, we checked out a motel that was for sale on the spectacular Thousand Islands archipelago straddling the Canada–U.S. border along the Saint Lawrence River. We hoped it would be a good location for the Wellness Center, but we were disappointed by its gloomy atmosphere—it was not what we were looking for, but we spent the night anyway.

When we gathered for breakfast in the morning, something was different about Ghanshyam; he was pensive, with a strange smile on his face and a faraway, almost trancelike look in his eyes.

"I had an incredible dream last night and I haven't fully recovered from it yet," he began. "I was standing in a beautiful meadow with sunshine streaming down all around me when I suddenly began to levitate. *Wow*, I thought, *I'm levitating! How about that!*

"Then I turned in midair and saw Lord Vishnu floating behind me. I knew it was Him—he looked exactly as he is pictured in so many portraits: refined features, blue skin, wearing a discus on his Jupiter finger and holding a conch shell representing the five elements of existence. But still, I could not believe my eyes and had to ask, 'Vishnu … is that you?'

"Lord Vishnu put his finger to his lips, silently signaling me to shush, and then he communicated with me telepathically.

"'Follow me,' he said wordlessly, and we both levitated upward. I have never experienced such peace; I surrendered to the beauty of the moment. We moved through space until we were hovering high above a sparkling lake. The lake was in the middle of a pristine forest surrounded by low mountains and had a shoreline of golden, reddish sand.

"'Do you love this place?' Vishnu asked me.

"'Oh, yes!' I answered. 'How could I not love it? It is a paradise!'

"Vishnu smiled at me, and then he was gone. And that was it—I woke up."

When Ghanshyam finished recounting his dream, we sat for a moment in silence, enthralled by the vividness of his story. Then Peter exclaimed, "Wow, Ghanshyam! That was quiet a dream!"

But I sensed it was not a dream, that Ghanshyam had experienced a vision.

When we got back to Montreal, there was a message on our answering machine from a realtor who had been searching for land for us.

"I think I finally found something you'll like. In fact, I'm sure you're going to love the place, it's a kind of paradise."

"This is going to be it," Ghanshyam said. "I know it is."

The property was an hour and half northwest of Montreal, just outside the small town of Chénéville, Quebec and not far from Mont-Tremblant, the world-famous ski resort in the Laurentian Mountains.

It was full-on winter when we visited Chénéville for the first time and, despite the bitter cold, it was impossible not to be awed by the beauty of the place—it was a winter wonderland. Sure enough, it was on a private lake, ringed by rolling, mountainous hills and surrounded by 500 acres of woodland forest. Although the lake was frozen over and covered in snow making it impossible to see if there was a shoreline of golden sand, everything matched what Vishnu showed Ghanshyam in the dream.

The Chénéville property had once been a spiritual retreat for Sulpician priests. Most recently, it had been known as Camp Cœur Joie (Happy Heart Camp), a summer camp for children. There were half a dozen buildings, most of them ramshackle and in dire need of a complete overhaul, but there was a large office, plenty of bedrooms in both the former priests' residence and the kids' bunkhouse, an industrial-sized kitchen in the main building with a huge cafeteria that could easily double as a lecture hall, and a deep well with clean, pure water.

As we were touring the grounds, we passed a stand of cedar trees concealing a small grotto. We looked up and beheld a life-sized statue of the Virgin Mary staring down at us, her arms opened in a gesture of welcome, her palms turned upward toward the sky.

"Mother Divine," Ghanshyam whispered reverently.

The prophetic words Bhrigu Nathulal spoke to Ghanshyam during his astrological reading in India a year before had suddenly taken form and materialized before our eyes.

You will establish a hast jyotish-related research institution and ashram, a school where people will come to study and stay and find food and shelter. There will be many buildings and a large property requiring much work. And there will be a statue of Mother Divine at this location—you are protected and supported and inspired to do great things there, by God's grace.

"I think I had better start filling out the paperwork," Ghanshyam whispered again. "It seems we're destined to buy this place."

The size of the property was intimidating to a city girl like me—it was as big as a national park—but none of us could disagree with Ghanshyam's pronouncement: destiny had brought us here. And when we returned after the snow melted in the spring, we were able get a clear view of the lake's shoreline and its beach of reddish, golden sand.

The visions, dreams and prophecies were followed by the lawyers; after half a year of legal negotiations, we finally purchased the Chénéville property, on June 22, 1998, and began creating our Wellness Center.

Following a flurry of activity, the first of the buildings was ready for occupancy on August 19, Ghanshyam's 57th birthday. The next day Peter drove Ghanshyam up north to spend his first official night at the Chénéville site. Almost everyone from the Center was up there working on the property, fixing up the kitchen and classroom, clearing the beach for swimming, building the massage studio and preparing the lodge for guests.

Kathy and I stayed behind in Montreal—we had students in town from California and China and regular clients and media appearances to tend to and we were racing to finish the final draft of *Love in the Palm of Your Hand* to meet our publication deadline.

We were so busy that we were sleeping in the office, and so preoccupied that we failed to heed the foreboding omens around us the day that Ghanshyam and Peter left for Chénéville—a large murder of crows incessantly cawed at the front of our building and we had a sudden infestation of spiders and ants—when added together, they warned of imminent danger.

Sometime after midnight, we called it a day. Kathy went to sleep on a cot in the backroom and I bedded down on blankets in my office. I woke up around 2 a.m. to the sound of Kathy's voice urgently calling my name as she knelt beside me, trying to shake me out of my deep slumber. I opened my eyes and was confused by the soft orange haze radiating at the back of the Center. Then I smelled the smoke. I jumped to my feet and instinctively headed toward the Handprint Gallery to grab whatever I could save. Kathy caught me by the arm.

"There's no time to get anything, Guylaine. The building is on fire—we have to get out of here," she said in a firm, but remarkably calm tone.

I turned and looked back at my Hanuman statue.

"*Now*, Guylaine, we have to get out of here *now*!

We made our way outside and stood in the middle of the street in our pajamas and bare feet as the flames shot up the back of the building. A few minutes later, fire engines roared up the street, their deafening sirens echoing between the buildings, their spinning red lights casting everything in a hellish red glow.

A gut-wrenching chorus of barks and yowling rose up in the veterinarian hospital that was attached to our building and undergoing heavy renovations. One of the firefighters smashed the hospital's plate glass door with a metal bar and a pack of terrified dogs and cats leapt through the broken shards, scrambling into the road. The pitiful, high-pitched howling of the caged pets that could not escape grew even louder; I covered my ears, unable to listen.

Ladders swung over the top of the Center as more firefighters descended onto the roof, hacking through the shingled wood with heavy axes. They blasted jets of water through the windows;

the Center hissed liked a dying thing. I began to cry at the horrific scene and Kathy put her arm around me and said, "Guylaine, we have to be strong."

A neighbor let us use his phone and we called Keero and told him what was happening. He showed up at 3 a.m. with a couple of huge trench coats and two pairs of his size 13 sneakers for us to wear. We looked like a slapstick comedy team and would have laughed at ourselves if everything we had worked so hard to build was not disappearing in smoke and flame in front of us.

Denise, who lived in a nearby building, had heard the sirens and ran to see where the fire was—she was as devastated as we were when she saw it was the Center. She leaned into us and we stood together watching helplessly as the building burned. A crowd gathered, and when the TV news cameras arrived, we stepped into the shadows, too shocked and broken to share our sorrow with strangers.

By early morning, the fire was out. Friends and clients who had seen what happened on television began arriving to offer support and condolences. My Mom and André hadn't been able to reach me on the phone so they drove up from Valleyfield to make sure we were okay.

When the restaurant next door opened for business that morning, I used their phone to call Ghanshyam in Chénéville and told him we had had a fire. He and Peter arrived a few hours later, and when they got out of the car, Ghanshyam was relieved to see us, and relieved to see that the front of the building was not severely damaged. But when we walked through the alley to the back of the building where the fire had been its worst, the Center was a gutted, burned-out shell. Ghanshyam's legs buckled; we caught him before he toppled over and wrapped our arms around him to hold him up. He burst into tears.

"Oh my God, I could have lost you. I could have lost you both," he sobbed, looking up to the second floor where we had been sleeping.

All we could see from where we stood was charred black wood, the white casing of Kathy's computer and the large poster of the saffron-robed Paramahansa, which had miraculously survived the blaze and had remained virtually untouched by the flames.

"What are we going to do, Ghanshyam?" I asked, too weak, weary and heartbroken to think ahead.

"What choice do we have?" he asked in return. "We will rebuild. We will carry on. That is what we are meant to do. It is what we must do."

CHAPTER 16

Staying Strong and Carrying On

*P*OLICE LOCKED DOWN THE Center and fire investigators sealed off the area with rolls of yellow tape. Our building was still smoldering hours later and no one was allowed to enter until the cause of the blaze was determined and the structure deemed safe. Luckily, Peter was born with an honest face and the Irish gift of the gab and convinced the fire marshal to let him slip into the Center for a couple of minutes. He emerged cradling Kathy's computer in his arms.

"It's a horrible mess in there," he reported to a half dozen of us, forlornly gathered at the edge of the police tape. "The sprinkler system came on and whatever wasn't burned was drenched—it looks like everything is ruined, all of it, everything. It's a miracle this computer survived."

It was a miracle all right—that computer contained our only copy of our *Love in the Palm of Your Hand* manuscript, which we had worked on for a year and a half and had all but completed.

Peter's description of the devastation hit us hard and we retreated to a nearby diner for an emergency meeting to discuss our immediate future. Kathy and I were still too dazed and tired to think or speak, so for the most part we sat and listened.

"We must say a prayer of thanks to God that we didn't lose anyone and that no one was hurt, because that's all that really matters," Ghanshyam said, looking at us with tears in his eyes. He bowed his head and fell silent for several moments. Save for the rattling of dishes coming from the diner's kitchen, we all sat together in complete silence.

"Okay, where are we now?" Ghanshyam continued. "We have lost our office, at least temporarily, but we haven't lost our mission. We have to carry on. We must push forward with the renovations at the Wellness Center, get our book published and find a new location to see clients and teach students until we get the Center up and running again. That could take a while, so I'm afraid we'll all have to take a pay cut until we're back on our feet financially."

Money was our biggest immediate concern. We had invested everything into the Wellness Center and recent renovations of the Center itself. We knew we could be tied up with the insurance company for months, maybe years, and with no place to teach or consult, we had no source of income. We did not even know if we could afford the lunch we had just ordered, let alone rent new office space.

"We can use my apartment as a new office," Denise said suddenly, offering up her home—just a five-minute walk from the Center—to save us from closing our doors. "I have a big two-bedroom but I'm happy to move into a studio apartment for a year, or however long it takes.

"We can set up a reception desk and office in the living room," she continued. "We can take handprints at the kitchen sink, use both bedrooms to do consultations … and the dining room is large enough to hold classes of 20 to 30 students. It might be a little cramped, but with a fresh coat of paint and some office furniture, it will be cozy and very professional looking."

"And anyone who can't afford to keep their own apartment," Johanne offered, in turn, "is more than welcome to stay with us as long as they like." She and Peter lived in the same apartment complex as Denise.

"Nuestra casa es su casa," Peter added. "Our house is your house."

"*Great!*" Ghanshyam said, with a big clap of his hands and a huge smile. "That's the spirit! That's beautiful. We'll start today! Let's contact all our clients and students and tell them where to find us and start fixing up Denise's place. A few of us can stay in Montreal to teach and do consultations and everybody else can head up to Chénéville to work on the Wellness Center. How about that!"

It was impossible not to be inspired by or admire Ghanshyam's resoluteness and enthusiasm—it was infectious. I leaned back in my chair and surveyed our little assembly of palmistry survivors. Many of our group who had traveled with us to India would find it too difficult to stay on with the Center in the coming months. The confusion and pay cut would prove too much and more than half the staff would leave to pursue other possibilities. But new and dedicated people like Jaysri and Rémi had joined us and would stay forever. The core group sitting together in the diner on the morning after the fire was strong, determined and united. I was heartened by the camaraderie I sensed among us at that moment—despite still being in shock from the tragedy we had just endured and daunted by the magnitude of the struggle we faced.

"This is going to be difficult," I said with a sigh, not realizing I was speaking aloud.

"Difficult? Sure, maybe," Rémi said, flashing his gap-toothed smile. "But everything is possible!" Like Ghanshyam, he was a man of unassailable optimism and I was happy to have him on the team.

A couple of days later, we were given access to the Center; it was worse than I had feared. The Handprint Gallery was destroyed, as was the large collection of rare *hast jyotish* books Ghanshyam and Kathy had assembled over the past quarter century. Everything was permeated with the reek of smoke and pigeons flew in and out of gaping holes that the firefighters had chopped into the roof. We spent days cleaning up the ruin. Peter and Rémi sloshed through pools of filthy water in knee-high rubber boots wearing protective masks as they shoveled chunks of burned plaster, splintered wood and broken glass into industrial garbage bags.

Insurance adjusters combed through the wreckage, ordering whatever was movable to be carted off for inventory at a suburban storage locker, where they would molder and rot for a year while Ghanshyam wrangled with our insurer over the claim. And a lot of our most prized possessions just mysteriously disappeared. Dealing with the insurance company proved more harrowing than the fire, which we were told had started in the veterinarian hospital adjacent to us. As our furniture was being hauled away I quietly tucked my Hanuman statue inside my jacket, then Kathy and I secured all our files and handprints before they could be confiscated and removed.

We bought a couple of clothes irons and used a little table in Denise's kitchen as an ironing board and began hot-pressing thousands of soggy documents and prints to prevent mold from setting in and to dry them enough to scan. It was a painstaking process and we labored like sweatshop laundresses, running on adrenaline for weeks after the fire. We ended up tossing most of the files into the garbage because they were too damaged to keep, but thankfully we were able to digitally preserve all of the beautiful handprints we had taken over the years.

The office phone and fax lines were transferred to Denise's and I started doing consultations there within days of the fire.

My first client at our new space reminded me that I was in the midst of a Mars *dasha*: she was a pretty, young, flame-haired exotic dancer at a Montreal strip club who went by the name of Chanel. She was eager to change career paths and after several consultations, she booked private palmistry lessons with me three times a week. Chanel wanted to become a palmist and seemed highly motivated and dedicated to learning palmistry and astrology. She was punctual and courteous and possessed a wry sense of humor that made me laugh; we had a really good time together. She was intelligent and picked up the basics very quickly; she even studied Vedic philosophy during her cigarette breaks at the strip club.

Then, one day, she showed up in an extremely combative mood. She opened my closet door and began rifling through my clothing.

"What's all this?" she shouted, and stomped into the kitchen, flinging open the fridge door.

"And what's with all this food? Do you *live* here?" she demanded, charging toward me. I moved behind my desk.

"You're teaching these classes illegally! Look at this place! This is your home, not a school! How do I know I'll even get a legitimate diploma when I graduate?"

"Chanel, I told you, the Center is being renovated after the fire and we're …"

"I don't care what you told me. Give me my money back right now. I want every cent I've given to you. Give my money, *now*!"

It was the most hostile outburst I had experienced in my dozen years of practicing palmistry. I was under attack and it took me a minute to collect myself.

Remain calm and professional; try to help her, I told myself and took a few long, deep breaths.

"Listen, Chanel, let's talk about what's bothering you. If you are dissatisfied and don't want to continue with the classes, I'm happy to contact the director about refunding your tuition. I'm really sorry you're unhappy and I wish …"

"*You're* the one that's going to be sorry, Guylaine. If I don't get my money soon, my boyfriend is going to come here to collect, and he's going to break both of your legs!"

She stormed out and slammed the door behind her.

I was saddened by what happened. I believed she really wanted to change her life. She had been gaining a better understanding of her past, herself and her current situation through palmistry, but something had derailed her resolve. I had a strong intuition that her manager—or, for all I knew, her pimp!—was worried about losing her money-making abilities and had pressured her to quit her efforts at self-improvement.

Chanel's boyfriend never showed up and my legs remained intact. We refunded her tuition anyway, but I kept her prints, which spoke volumes about her life. Her destiny line terminated at her very short head line, which told me that her shortsighted way of thinking was sabotaging her future. And the huge phalange on her thumb representing her will, combined with her large Mars negative, bore out what I had personally witnessed: she was prone to rash decision-making and sudden outbursts of negativity, anger and violence. But I was certain her lines and her life would have changed had she devoted herself to palmistry for a little while longer. It was a shame. I still think of Chanel, hoping she broke free of her troubled environment and altered the course of her destiny. None of us is a prisoner of our fate, but it takes effort if we hope to outwit the stars.

Fortunately, not one of our other students or clients ever complained about our temporary location. But my encounter with Chanel had been so disquieting, I wondered about the role Mars was playing in my life that drew her troubled and negative energy to me. I began carrying a picture of Hanuman in my wallet—I wanted to feel protected by his strength and feel his courage at all times during the remaining five years of my Mars *dasha*.

Not long after that unpleasant confrontation, the final version of *Love in the Palm of Your Hand* went to the printers. Our American publisher called the office from Vermont.

"I love the book," he said. "And I think it could sell very well with the right promotion—unfortunately, we have no promotional budget at all, but I strongly urge you to do your own book tour."

Despite our overstretched finances, it was important for us to get our first book out into the world. We all agreed to tighten our belts once again to finance a book tour that would take Ghanshyam, Kathy and Peter across the U.S. and Canada. Because Ghanshyam was deathly afraid of flying, they would travel by road in Peter's old Subaru. They set off in January 1999 on what was supposed to be a three-month tour, but the tour was more successful than we could have imagined. We began making major inroads into the U.S. and developing clients in communities we never imagined reaching.

The 90-day book tour became a six-year odyssey that took our roving band of palmistry crusaders up and down the Eastern Seaboard between Maine to Miami, and back and forth across Central Canada, the U.S. Midwest, Southwest and Deep South. They spent months at a time living out of their suitcases and preparing Indian meals on hotplates in economy motel rooms. They crisscrossed and re-crisscrossed the continent promoting *Love in the Palm of Your Hand* and introducing *hast jyotish* to America, one palm at a time.

The tour divided our already reduced staff into three teams—the Chénéville team, who were building the Wellness Center; the Montreal team, responsible for teaching classes, conducting client consultations and overseeing the renovation of the burned-out Center; and our mobile team, responsible for promoting the book. To finance the never-ending book tour and keep the mobile team self-sufficient, Johanne ran central command in Chénéville and—in-between manning the reception desk, cooking for Wellness Center guests, translating *Love in the Palm* into French and seeing her own clients—she coordinated lectures, appearances at esoteric trade shows and private readings for the three mobile team members in each city they passed through.

They would return home periodically for short visits and to load up with more books before taking to the highway again. We ensured they never ran out of inventory by writing and publishing two more books during their U.S. tour: *Magnet Therapy* (with our friend, gemologist Colette Hemlin) and *Destiny in the Palm of Your Hand*, the companion follow-up to *Love in the Palm of Your Hand*, which illustrated how to shape your personal destiny through palmistry.

Being separated from Kathy and Ghanshyam, my devoted teachers and mentors, for such a protracted period was difficult for me. I had come to rely on their constant companionship and all that accompanied that closeness—moral support, encouragement, deep friendship and sound advice. Denise and Johanne were dear friends, as well as being amazing, hardworking coworkers, but without the immediate lifeline of Ghanshyam and Kathy, I was on my own more often than I had been in years. And I was forced to become more self-reliant, both personally and professionally. It was not an easy time, but it pushed me beyond my established boundaries, made me delve deeper into my craft and provided an opportunity for me to give back and prove my devotion to my friends, my teachers and my cause.

I was the senior staff member while the others were away and responsible for whatever happened at the Center. We were very short-staffed, so everyone was working double-duty and had to remain highly focused on their particular tasks.

One of my own new duties was teaching Kathy's and Ghanshyam's classes while they were on the road, including Ghanshyam's classes in advanced astrology. He had been teaching astrology for 30 years and I had never taught it before in my life!

To prepare me, Ghanshyam would record his lectures while driving across the States, then FedEx the tapes to me whenever he arrived at a sizable town. The recordings invariably reached me at the last minute the day before the class, and I would stay up the entire night transcribing and studying.

Something also new to me was acting as a foreman to deal with the contractors and workers renovating the Center in Montreal. Tours of the worksite became a regular part of my routine over the two years it took to repair and remodel our main offices. Meanwhile, I had frequent radio and television appearances to do, private classes to teach, and my own consultation clientele, which nearly doubled in size when the *Claire Lamarche* show I had appeared on in 1996 was rebroadcast.

The Happy Palmist

I frequently did eight consultations a day and, with my teaching and other duties, was often putting in 80-hour weeks. I was definitely not getting enough sleep, a condition exacerbated by the constant jarring clamor from construction going on next-door to Denise's apartment. I certainly did not need an alarm clock—for an entire year I was woken at dawn every morning by the bone-rattling, machine-gun pounding of jackhammers, which droned in my ears all day and into the evening. The assault and battery on my system frayed my nerves and I am amazed none of my clients ever mentioned it, even when I had to shout to be heard during a reading or a class.

Each night, I would collapse into bed at 10 or 11 p.m. and call the mobile team to see how their day had gone. It was good to hear their inspiring progress reports from New York City, Boston, Honolulu or Sedona, or wherever in the world they were. I was so exhausted I would often fall asleep with the phone in my hand listening to their cheery voices.

On the weekends, Denise and I would drive up to help the Chénéville team. They were laboring away, reroofing the buildings, clearing forest and beaver dams, digging wells and landscaping the magnificent grounds. I would do consultations there on Saturdays and then spend long hours on Sunday afternoons stripping and repainting the truckloads of Salvation Army furniture we had purchased to furnish the Wellness Center. It was hard work, but seeing our country health retreat slowly take shape was the most rejuvenating therapy any doctor could have prescribed, and, other than my morning meditation and daily Kriya Yoga, it was my only respite from a relentless schedule I was locked into.

One crisp February day, I was overseeing a promotional shoot at the Wellness Center to advertise a Valentine Special we were planning. We had a photographer shooting the gorgeous surroundings and needed a couple of models to act like they were in love—Denise and Rémi volunteered. Rémi got down on his knee and proposed to Denise, and would not get up until she said yes. The impatient photographer yelled, "Hey, quit your fooling around!"

"Who's fooling?" Rémi said, and with that, he proposed to Denise again. It was the beginning of a beautiful relationship. Considering that Rémi and Denise have been together ever since and did get married, they are our most successful Valentine Special to date. For me, their happiness was a joyful portent into the future we envisioned for the Wellness Center—a place to celebrate life and love, a place to focus on what is most important, a place to dream of what is possible and a place where dreams come true. It was a wonderful day.

As were the days when Kathy, Ghanshyam and Peter returned to Montreal every five or six months with their suitcases jammed full with gifts and their hearts and heads filled with stories of their adventures. I was always so happy when we were all together, and proud of the part I was playing in helping to bring Vedic palmistry to the wider world. I hated to see the mobile team leave again, but always remembered what my mom used to say during the decade Dad spent away from home working in New York State: "Our love doesn't go away; we always find our way back together and are stronger than ever. So long as there is love, everything is fine!"

And everything was fine, although I was anxious about keeping it that way. Anxiety was one of my "12 flaws" that still crept up on me and that I was still working to rid myself of. During that hectic period of life I picked up bad eating habits to help me cope. What can I say—potato chips are my go-to comfort food! Before I knew it, I had gained 20 pounds. I was unhappy that some of my clothes no longer fit, but I came to think of the extra weight as my "Mars Warrior fat"—a little extra padding to protect me from the troubles and suffering that often accompany a Mars *dasha*. And I would need all the protection I could get. Mars in the 11th house, as mine was, could indicate difficulty with elder brothers, and the difficulty coming to me was devastating.

On September 19, 1999, I was doing an out-of-town consultation at the home of longtime clients when their phone rang in the middle of the reading. When they told me the call was for me, I knew it could not be good news. It was my brother Gaston.

"Guylaine, how soon can you get to Valleyfield? André is in the hospital ... he's in a coma. He had a brain aneurysm. It doesn't look good."

"I'm on my way," I said, and hung up the phone.

Oh God, no! Not André! I thought as I apologized to my clients and walked out the door halfway through their reading. I loved all my brothers equally, but André, Mimi and I were the youngest and had a special bond. As kids we were like the Three Musketeers—all for one and one for all, and that closeness had never died.

A few hours later, I arrived at André's hospital room just as a priest was walking in. Mimi and Réjean were already there and we hugged each other.

"We sent Mom home to sleep. She is really shaken up," Mimi sobbed. "The doctors are still running tests, but they say we should be prepared for the worst. They can't even tell us if he's going to wake up. We'll leave you with him for a few minutes."

She and Réjean left the room and I took my sweet brother's hand in mine, hoping he could hear my voice deep within his coma.

"André, it's Guylaine. I love you. I always have and I always will."

The priest was standing on the other side of the bed. He made the sign of the cross over André, smeared oil onto his eyelids and began speaking in Latin.

"*Per istam Sanctam unctionem et suam Piissimam misericordiam, indulgeat tibi Dominus quidquid deliquisti ...*"

Oh no. He was giving André the Last Rites and I knew that my brother was going to die. I bent down and kissed his face, hugging him as tightly as I could. A few minutes later, a group of doctors wheeled André away somewhere so they could be ready to harvest his organs when the time came. It was what André had requested, to help others through his death. He died a few hours later without ever regaining consciousness.

There was a slow burning anger in the pit of my stomach. Why had God taken this loving, kind man away from us and from his teenage son, Martin? André was so young himself—just 46, in the prime of his life and with so much to offer. To be cut down by something as random as a brain aneurysm—it seemed so unfair, to him, to us—and to my mother, whom we woke up in the middle of the night with the news that one of her boys had died. She climbed out of bed in a trance, as though she had not heard or could not acknowledge what we had told her. She took two or three steps then collapsed on the floor and began wailing: "Oh no! Not my baby, not my baby!"

Seeing and hearing my mother's pain ripped another hole in my heart.

Ghanshyam, Kathy and Peter returned from the road to join the rest of the gang from the Center at the funeral. Ghanshyam picked up on my anger and invited me to join them on the next leg of the tour in Kingston, Ontario, and I did. It was good to be around them, and after one of the book signings, he took me aside and gave some tender advice.

"I know you are angry about what happened to André. That's natural. But it is what we choose to do with our anger that makes all the difference in our lives. The noble warrior uses his anger to protect those he loves; the spiteful warrior lets his anger fester and turns it inward. He hurts himself and the people he most cares about. Use your pain and anger to empathize with your clients. Grief is not a virtue. We all suffer loss—use your suffering to help others."

I remembered Ghanshyam's advice two years later when I received another urgent call. It was September 11, 2001 and I was a guest on the popular Montreal TV morning show *Deux filles le matin* (Two Girls in the Morning), when the hijacked planes flew into the twin towers of the World Trade Center in Manhattan.

We watched the horror unravel on television. When I left the studio, I went from mourning with the world to mourning a very personal tragedy. I got a phone call from Mimi about my brother Marcel—he had terminal lung cancer and was not expected to survive the week.

Once again, I found myself in a Valleyfield hospital room with one of my brothers. Marcel looked like a sweet child in the big bed and I sat with him for hours telling him how much I loved him as he promised to get better so we could spend more time together.

He passed away the next day with Mom and Mimi at his side, his life of suffering and depression coming to a peaceful end surrounded by love. He was 50 and the second child my mother had to bury; the pain was taking a heavy toll on her.

At Marcel's funeral, I let go of my anger, just as Marcel had taught me to so many years before when I was a bitter and confused teenager blaming him for my unhappiness and shortcomings. I said a silent prayer of thanks to him for the great gift he had given me, for setting me on the path of becoming a better person, and I promised to share that gift through my work for the rest of my life. And I prayed that he had found his own peace and happiness at long last.

My Mars *dasha* dealt me one more painful family blow before it ended. Six or seven months after Marcel died, my brother Gaston phoned me in Montreal.

"Monique's been diagnosed with cancer. She's going to get treatment but it's already spread." Gaston and Monique started dating when I was a kid. I had been the ring bearer at their wedding and over the years she had become a big sister to me. Seeing my brother and his children so deeply distressed was unbearable. She was in great pain for many months, and was finally released from her suffering a year after her diagnosis. Gaston cared for Monique every day and was with her when she passed. Mom cried so much, I don't think she had any more tears left in her increasingly fragile body.

On December 15, 2002, my Mars *dasha* finally ended. It had been a grueling, difficult and often painful seven-year period, but I had learned so much, stretched and tested myself, and had overcome some enormous obstacles as well as played a role in some great achievements. The rebuilding and remodeling of the Palmistry Center in Montreal was complete and it was even more beautiful than before.

The Wellness Center in Chénéville was now open for business and it was one of the most glorious retreats I had ever seen. We created trails for nature walks and opened a private beach for swimming in one of the cleanest lakes in Quebec. Work was still being finished there on the yoga and meditation complex, but our lakeside lodge was completed and Jaysri and Rémi were giving Ayurvedic massages in one of our two new massage studios. And one of my most devoted palmistry students, a tall, strapping former firefighter named Francis Desjardins, was training to become our third massage therapist.

Things were looking up. The Center was being regularly featured in the media, we had published three successful books, we had not lost a single client due to the fire and we were rapidly expanding our clientele in the United States.

Christmas was coming and I wanted to take a deep breath, put my feet up and take a break to enjoy all the gains made during my long, turbulent *dasha*. But when the mobile team returned to Montreal for the holidays, Ghanshyam had other ideas. "Guylaine, I want you to go get an American work visa."

"What on earth for, Ghanshyam? I've just finished building up a great group of clients here!"

"Don't worry about that. Pack your bags—you're moving to Miami."

CHAPTER 17

In the Sunshine State

FLORIDA IS A NICE place to visit, but I did not want to live there.

I was happy in Montreal, where I was close to my family, surrounded by friends I loved and clients and students who relied on me. In December 2002, my consultation calendar was already booked up, and I was preparing to teach a new series of classes. The money I brought in went straight back to the Center and was much needed after years of repairs, renovations and expansion. It boggled my mind that Ghanshyam wanted to send Peter and me to Miami to start up a new branch office in a city where I did not have a single client. As far as I was concerned, I would be most useful to the Center right where I was and I did not want to leave.

Ghanshyam did not see it that way. He gained a following in Miami during his book tours and possessed a list of potential clients for us. There was also a trade show on alternative health care in Miami on January 5, which was Paramahansa's birthday, and Ghanshyam believed having a presence at the event on such an auspicious date would lead us to a sizable Miami clientele. He rented us a booth at the trade show and arranged for Peter and me to go down to Florida before the trade show started in order to get the lay of the land and use his list to set up consultations with clients.

But, after everything we had been through recovering from the fire, it did not make sense to me to gamble with what we had rebuilt and send me away for several months, and I told Ghanshyam how I felt.

"Don't worry so much," he assured me. "You have my client list, you have the trade show and you have Peter—it will be fine. This will be good for you. And don't forget to take some time to relax and enjoy the sunshine while you are there."

I wish I could have relaxed and shared his enthusiasm. But I grew increasingly anxious about the move. On the eve of our departure, I again urged Ghanshyam to reconsider.

"This is crazy, Ghanshyam! Things are good as they are. I'm earning a lot and I'm comfortable here. I know everybody and everybody knows me. Why risk losing that by sending me to Miami? It's not logical. Besides, 60% of the population in Miami is Hispanic, and the only thing I can say in Spanish is *mañana*—tomorrow!"

"*Good!*" Ghanshyam said, with a big smile. "You see, you are already learning the lingo! So get a good night's sleep—you're leaving *mañana*!"

It was pointless arguing with Ghanshyam once he had made up his mind about something, and he had decided that Peter and I would be the Center's first ambassadors to the Sunshine State.

On December 30, 2002, exactly seven years to the day that we had embarked on our India adventure, we loaded our hand printing equipment and summer clothing into Peter's Subaru, pushed the car out of a snowbank and set off on the 2,600-kilometer journey.

The weather was as gloomy as my mood. It was dark and overcast when we crossed the U.S. border and we drove through freezing rain, snow and fog in Vermont, New York and Virginia. By the time we had reached the Carolinas, though, my spirits were beginning to lift. I turned off the car's heater, rolled down the window and let the warm wind blow through my hair. When we pulled into Miami, my toes were tapping to the Latin rhythms blasting from car radios on the street. I loved the brightness, the tropical heat, the exotic palm trees and the soothing echo of ocean waves breaking against the golden shore.

This could turn out to be a nice working holiday, I thought. But while Miami would be many things to us, it would not be a vacation.

We had arranged to stay with our friend Grace, a colleague at the Center who recently retired and was now living in West Palm Beach, which is about an hour north of Miami. Grace generously invited us to stay with her until we established a clientele and were able to rent a place to live and do consultations.

At the time, Peter and I—along with our colleagues in Montreal—were practicing a yearlong meditation program called *Purusha* (Sanskrit for "self"). *Purusha* is intended to develop our intuition, focus and magnetism, and introduce us to our higher self. In addition to adding an extra half-hour of mantras to our morning meditation by reciting the 108 sacred names of Mother Divine, the *Purusha* required us to give up certain physical enjoyments, like eating meat, drinking alcohol and sleeping in a bed. It was a rigorous program, but one that offered powerful spiritual rewards.

It was a fortuitous coincidence to be in the middle of a *Purusha* when we arrived in Florida—we were on such an extremely tight budget we could not afford liquor or meat, and Grace did not have much extra space in her small condo, so Peter and I had to sleep on the floor anyway.

Despite my extra meditation, I was nervous about our finances both in Florida and back at the Center. As soon as we arrived at Grace's I began calling the clients Ghanshyam had seen when he was in Miami. Unfortunately, the clients on Ghanshyam's list were eager to see Ghanshyam, not us.

"Nice talking to you, but please call back when Dr. Birla is in Miami" was the mantra repeated to me over and over from the other end of the phone. I crossed names off the list until there was no one left to call.

"What are we going to do now?" I asked Peter.

"Not to worry, we've got a few days before the groceries run out," Peter said, with his usual peppy and easygoing optimism. He was a perfect traveling companion; he never complained and his good humor and calmness balanced the scales next to my anxiety and fretting.

"But we've got to do *something*!"

"Okeydoke," Peter said. That afternoon, he drove his Subaru all over Miami and West Palm Beach and left our card and brochure at every spiritual center, yoga studio, health food store, doughnut shop and gas station he could find. That night, we sat by the phone waiting for it to ring. It did not.

Over the next several days, we visited local libraries and gave free lectures on Vedic palmistry and astrology to small but enthusiastic gatherings, hoping to drum up business that way.

"Don't forget to tell your friends about us," we encouraged the patrons. "We're available for private and group consultations anytime—call us in the next 48 hours and we'll give you a special discount!"

The phone still did not ring. I called Ghanshyam in a panic.

"Peter and I are practically begging people to show us their hands. We called everyone on your list but no one is interested in seeing us—we don't have a single paying customer lined up!"

"Don't worry so much, Guylaine," Ghanshyam reassured me. "Be patient, have faith, meditate and pray. We aren't selling palmistry, we're offering hope. People will come."

Ghanshyam's confidence settled me down, for a while. But after more days of fruitless self-promotion, I was ready to give up. The evening before the health trade show, Peter and I went to a restaurant and treated ourselves to a *Purusha* special—a vegetarian burger and non-alcoholic beer.

"As far as I'm concerned, it's hopeless here," I said. "If the health trade show is a bust tomorrow, we should head straight to the freeway and start driving north. Do you agree?"

"Agreed. Tomorrow is D-day," Peter said, and raised his drink in the air. We clinked our bottles of boozeless beer and toasted our imminent departure.

When we got back to Grace's, I made my nightly call to Ghanshyam and told him of our decision.

"Well then, you mustn't forget to meditate and pray tomorrow morning," Ghanshyam said sweetly.

The next morning we got up early and meditated for nearly two hours before heading off to the convention center. It was a beautiful, sunny, Sunday morning and the beaches were already crowded with families and sun worshippers. *Who is going to want to be inside on a gorgeous day like this?* I thought. And I was right—the convention center was virtually empty and only a couple of people passed by our booth the entire morning. At noon, I phoned Ghanshyam yet again.

"That's it, Ghanshyam. The trade show is a complete washout. Nobody's here. We're leaving right now. We'll pack up and be in Montreal by tomorrow night!"

"Settle down, Guylaine," Ghanshyam said calmly. "Give it one more hour."

"*Honestly*, Ghanshyam! What difference will an hour make? The place is empty!"

"Please, just wait one more hour and you'll see. Okay?"

"Okay, Ghanshyam, but at one o'clock, we're out of here."

I sat in our booth impatiently for the next 58 minutes, checking my watch every few seconds. Not a single person came to see us. At 12:59 p.m., I looked at Peter.

"Time to leave," I said. Then I heard a voice behind me.

"Excuse me, dear, can you tell me what these three lines on my wrist mean?"

I turned around to find a very well-groomed, sharply dressed middle-aged woman with short blonde hair holding her right wrist out toward me.

"I've asked quite a few palmists if these lines have any significance," she continued, "but it seems to be a mystery to all of them."

The woman was with a friend and I invited them to have a seat in our booth.

"I'll be happy to explain them to you," I said, taking her hand and pointing to the three horizontal lines spanning her wrist. "These are called bracelets—the top line closest to your hand is your wisdom bracelet, the middle is wealth and the one furthest from your hand is health. They correspond to our body, mind and soul. Not everyone is as fortunate to have all three bracelets, as you have."

"Finally!" she said excitedly. "A palmist who knows what they're talking about!"

I leaned in for a closer look at her hand and my attention was captured by her lines. As I focused on them, my stress and urgency to make a quick getaway vanished. I was doing what I loved doing most—reading a palm.

"Wow, you have a very pronounced wisdom bracelet—one of the deepest I've ever seen," I said, looking up at her. "A really fascinating thing about these bracelets is that they are located on the Mount of Ketu, which is strongly associated with Karma. The rishis—the divinely inspired seers of ancient India—believed that the bracelets on Ketu reveal a lot about our past life and present Karma. The most pronounced bracelet tells us what was most important to us in our past lives, as well as the Karma we're working on in this life."

"Oh really! So does my deep wisdom bracelet mean I am a very wise woman, then?" she laughed.

"It just might!" I smiled, turning back to her hand. "Your wrist is also very delicate and narrow. Your fingers are supple and your hand is long, rectangular and graceful. And look at this strong Mount of Luna. You have quite a rare hand—we call it a 'psychic hand.' You're probably quite intuitive."

She gave me a long, quizzical stare for several seconds, and then asked, "Do you have time to do a reading for me and my friend right now?"

"Of course!" I said.

I did her reading and Peter read her friend's palm. They were both very happy with their consultations and when we were done, she handed me her business card: *Frances Fox, Psychic Medium*.

"You guys are terrific! I give a big lecture in a luxury hotel downtown every Friday night. It's always packed—the address is on the card. From now on, I want the two of you to set up a table and do audience readings after the show. Charge whatever you want—everyone is going to love you," she said, as she walked off into the empty convention center.

Peter and I looked at each other in shock.

"Well, how about that?" Peter chuckled, using Ghanshyam's favorite phrase. "Ghanshyam was right about waiting."

"What else is new, Peter?" I said, shaking my head in amazement while looking down at my own Mount of Ketu. I wondered what Karma I had collected in my past lives that made me so impatient in this one. I had a lesson to learn here in Miami, and Ghanshyam must have known that.

The next day, we heeded Ghanshyam's earlier advice and finally took an afternoon off to enjoy some sunshine. We headed for the beach—it had been a stressful few days and I needed to reconnect with nature, relax and recharge my batteries. Peter loved swimming in the sea and plunged into the surf the moment we got there. I preferred basking in the sun. I lay down on the warm sand and let the energizing rays seep into my soul. Meeting Frances Fox at the moment Ghanshyam predicted I would find clients made me reflect on the past couple of weeks and why I had resisted coming to Miami.

I was very comfortable in Montreal. Even when the worst happened—the death of loved ones or the Center burning down—I could count on the gang for support and to keep me calm. But, aside from Peter's great company, I was on my own in Miami.

In Montreal, people called *me* for consultations. I had never had to start from scratch and hunt for clients before. Amidst all the uncertainty, my old nemesis—my anxiety—resurfaced. I had a renewed appreciation for what Ghanshyam had accomplished when he first arrived in Canada without money or speaking the language. With his faith, devotion and passion, he was able to draw clients to him and build both the Palmistry and the Wellness Centers. I had more than a sneaking suspicion that he had sent me to Miami to learn to do the same. Anxiety was an anchor that had kept me from taking risks, having faith in myself and the universe, and going with the flow of life. It was an anchor I did not want in my life again.

As I had been so many times in the past, I was grateful to have a teacher as wise as Ghanshyam and grateful that we were doing a *Purusha* program—maybe I was meeting my higher self in Miami, of all places.

On the Friday night, we went to the hotel where Frances was speaking and set up our table. There were several hundred people in the audience and Frances received thunderous applause when she stepped onto the stage. Apparently, she was very well known in Miami. Choosing people from the audience at random, she revealed specific details about their past, present and future. She effortlessly switched between Spanish and English during her readings as she captivated, enthralled and entertained everyone with her dynamic presence and predictions. I remembered being impressed by her big Sun mount and long Sun line when I looked at her palm days earlier, which I knew was the source of amazing magnetism and charisma.

After she wrapped up for the evening and took her final bow, she pointed toward the lobby where Peter and I were sitting.

"Ladies and gentlemen. *Señoras y señores*. Your fate is not sealed! *Su destino no está sellado!* The lines of your hand can change! *Las líneas de la mano pueden cambiar!*

"Tonight we have two great palmists with us who can tell you how to change your lines, and change your destiny! They read

The Happy Palmist

my palm the other day and I can tell you, they are fantastic! Go and see them!"

People poured out of the auditorium and formed a long line at our table. We had so many clients, we did not have time to take prints; we read palm after palm as they thrust them in front of us and worked for hours without pause. One of our customers ran a busy Miami Pilates studio and was so pleased with her consultation that she invited us to come to her studio every week to do readings for her clients.

Frances dropped by our table on her way home. "I told you they would love you," she said with a wink. "See you next week!"

A couple of days later, Grace and Jeannette, a new mutual friend, introduced me to a group of their West Palm Beach neighbors interested in learning palmistry and I started a weekly introductory class.

Not long after that, we got a phone call from Zide Mooni, a highly successful Miami acupuncturist of East Indian descent who was a good friend and client of Ghanshyam and had just found out we were in town. "Welcome to Florida, Guylaine," Zide said. "I love palmistry, I love Ghanshyam and I'm going to make you famous in Miami."

Zide was a real character—a big, strong, confident man with an enormous heart to match his impressive frame. Everyone adored him and so did we—he introduced us to a couple hundred of his patients and many of his friends and family—all of whom became new clients for us.

As always, Ghanshyam had been so, so right; we offered hope and the people surely did come.

Peter and I became so busy we had little time for anything other than meditation, work and a few hours of sleep. But we were doing what we loved, so we were having fun despite our suddenly hectic schedule. From Monday to Friday, we worked with clients in West Palm Beach. On Friday afternoons, we drove to Miami for our regular gig reading palms after Frances's hotel performance. On Saturdays, we met up with Zide at his office and did 10 hours of consultations with the clients he had lined up for us—then, after a catnap on the office floor, we would get up at dawn on Sunday and do another 10 hours of consultations. We would drive back to West Palm Beach on Sunday night and start our weekly routine again Monday morning.

Once a week, as per Ghanshyam's advice, we dropped everything for a few hours and went to the beach to decompress and reenergize. After all, what Canadian can resist basking in the hot Florida sun in the middle of winter?

I was determined to go with the flow of life—and I found the more I shed my anxiety, the more opportunity opened up to me. We were invited to do consultations all over South Florida—we did readings in Key West, the southernmost point in the continental U.S., drove across Alligator Alley from Fort Lauderdale on the Atlantic Coast to the sugar-white beaches of Clearwater on the Gulf of Mexico. We visited the Everglades, attended the Miami Philharmonic Symphony and danced at a bar owned by Madonna in South Beach, where we met and did a consultation with a jazz musician who loved the Gayatri Mantra. And wherever we went, we were accompanied by the cool strains of Sting and Céline Dion, whose discs were constantly spinning in the Subaru's CD player—our personal Florida soundtrack.

We were so busy, we sometimes recruited help from the Montreal and Chénéville teams—Jaysri and Denise. In late spring of 2003, Ghanshyam came down with Kathy and Johanne and set up a booth at the Silva Method Convention where Ghanshyam was a guest lecturer, and Dr. Wayne Dyer, one of our favorite inspirational authors, was the keynote speaker. Kathy had consulted the astrological charts before coming down and discovered that several planets were exalted in the sky that May, which made it a very auspicious time for meeting someone special. And, sure enough, Wayne passed by our booth and began asking questions about what we did. He was so intrigued by the spiritual roots of Vedic palmistry that he had me ink his palms and take his prints right then and there. His long fingers pointed to his deeply philosophical nature and a strong love of truth line showed his desire to delve into the mysteries of life. He also had a balanced quadrangle, which is formed by the head and heart lines and is often referred to as the "landing strip of the angels," which told us he was receptive to the wisdom of great teachers and visionary dreams.

A dozen years later, we met Wayne again in Ottawa and redid his prints. He saw for himself that our lines truly do change—his palms reflected a deep spiritual growth in those 12 years, which, not surprisingly, corresponded to his growing interest in Vedic philosophy, Kriya Yoga and the practice of daily meditation.

Wayne was not the only "special" person we met during that period of unique planetary alignment. That same week, we were invited to the home of Puerto Rican pop star Ricky Martin. Ricky was living in a posh suburb north of Miami, and when he heard about Ghanshyam through a friend of Zide, he sent word that he wanted a reading.

The whole gang ended up at Ricky's palatial, oceanside mansion, where he greeted us wearing shorts, a T-shirt and a big smile. We chatted a bit and discovered that he was also a follower of Paramahansa, practiced Kriya Yoga every day and had a love of Vedic philosophy. Kathy took his prints and he went off with Ghanshyam to another room for a private, three-hour reading.

As Peter, Johanne, Kathy and I waited, we analyzed and admired the lines and signs we had seen in Ricky's hands. He had an incredibly beautiful Venus, which was the most prominent mount in his hand and accounted for his passionate love of music as well as his deep commitment to philanthropic work. His perfectly rounded life line revealed his joie de vivre—which the entire world heard expressed in his irresistibly upbeat megahit "Livin' La Vida Loca."

In many ways, I myself had been living *la vida loca* (a crazy life) since arriving in Miami. I had spent months overcoming obstacles and challenges within myself to establish our new branch office in a foreign country, and I had made progress both professionally and personally. I guess Ghanshyam thought so, too.

In the car after leaving Ricky Martin's place, Ghanshyam turned to me with a smile.

"I told you this trip would be good for you, Guylaine," he said. "From now on, we can fly down to Miami to see our clients. It's time for you to come home to us."

I sighed with relief. I treasured my time in Miami, but was so very happy to be homeward bound. During my Florida adventure, I had discovered that the Sunshine State is not merely a destination; it is a state of mind.

CHAPTER 18

There's No Place Like Home

WHEN I RETURNED FROM Florida, I felt like Dorothy in *The Wizard of Oz*—I had had an amazing adventure but I was glad to be home. Ghanshyam, Kathy and Peter continued with the book tour for two more years, but, except for occasional excursions to consult with my clients in Miami and a few other major U.S. cities, I planted myself firmly on the home front. I had formed a powerful bond with my students and regular clients there and needed to be near them. I also did not want to stray far from my mother. Her spirit was as strong as ever, but time and grief had worn her body down and I wanted to see her as often as possible while I still could.

For years after my dad passed away, Mom refused to sell the big house he had built for us—partly because he had hidden so many little presents for her in its nooks and crannies that she could not bear to leave even one unfound; and partly because the house was close to Marcel's apartment. Marcel had struggled with daily life since his anguishing breakdown when I was a teenager and watching out for him had been Mom's mission. Now that Marcel was gone, Mom lost her sense of purpose and her energy began to wane. The big, empty house became too much for her to manage.

"The stairs seem to get steeper every day," she confided.

So we sold our beautiful home and found Mom a small apartment, but when even that became too demanding, she agreed it was time to move into an assisted-living facility.

Mom decorated her room with her usual artistic flair and turned it into a real home: hanging a handmade wreath on the door and enlivening the walls with the pictures she had painted over the years. And she kept a small fridge stocked with our favorite snacks so we always felt as though we were sitting in our family living room when we visited, not at an institution.

One day, in the fall of 2005, Mom collapsed and could not get up. She was transferred to the hospital, where the doctors gave us a grim prognosis: her heart was failing and it was unlikely she would survive the week. The news was as devastating as it was hard to believe. When I arrived in Valleyfield, I found Mom sitting up in her hospital bed with a big smile on her face, her sparkling blue eyes as bright and beautiful as ever.

"Hello, my sweet girl," she said happily. At 81, she was still so vibrant and youthful, I could not accept that her magnificent heart was giving out and her life had run its course.

Réjean, Gaston, Mimi and I took shifts at her side all week so she would not be alone; on her final night, Mimi and I were sitting on the bed with her.

"I love you too much to say goodbye," she said. "I can't bear to go on and leave you behind."

"Oh, Mom!" Mimi and I sobbed in unison. The three of us began weeping and reached for the box of tissues on the bedside table. Mom gently swatted our hands away.

"Don't use up all my tissues, I'll be all out!"

We broke out laughing.

"Oh my! I sure am going to miss you all. But at least I know I'll be leaving a lot of love behind in the world," Mom said, taking our hands in hers. "Your father and I loved each other so much; you kids are the beautiful product of that love."

When Mimi left the room to get us coffee, I leaned in a little closer to my mother.

There was something I had to ask her, now that we were alone.

"Mom, was I a good daughter to you?" I whispered. "I mean, did I ever hurt or disappoint you?"

Even though she had never said so, deep down I assumed Mom wished I had gotten married, had children and led a more normal life. It hurt me thinking I had let her down.

She looked at me with a puzzled smile and shook her head.

"What in the world are you talking about, you silly girl? You have been a wonderful daughter! Your father and I couldn't have been prouder of you. Because of you, we could brag we had a teacher in the family. You found your calling and have worked for a cause—you are helping people and I hope you never stop. You've made me very, very happy."

Tears streamed down my cheeks. Her words were a gift, the sweetest blessing I had ever received. I looked into her sweet blue eyes and I knew I would miss the love I saw shining through them for the rest of my life. A few hours later, she died peacefully in her sleep. My heart was broken, but I will always treasure our final moments together and the opportunity to express our love for each other one last time.

The entire gang from the Center drove down to Valleyfield and joined my family and 300 of Mom's friends in a final farewell to the beautiful Laurette. The love Mom so freely shared during her life was reflected in every face—her love would be her legacy and would live in the many hearts she had touched.

I was 45 when Mom passed and I began wondering what my own legacy would be. To help as many people as possible live happier, healthier lives through my teaching would be more than enough for me. I was deeply grateful to have taught the life-changing art of palmistry to hundreds of students already, but I intended to teach it to thousands. We had worked hard for years to have *hast jyotish* recognized as a serious field of study in the West, and before Mom died both the Quebec provincial and Canadian federal governments acknowledged that the Birla College of Vedic Palmistry was a bona fide educational institution, allowing students across the country to claim the cost of their tuition and textbooks on their tax returns. It meant the world to me that Mom lived long enough to see the mantle of legitimacy bestowed upon the Birla College and the work I did there.

After she passed away, I threw myself into teaching with renewed passion and conviction. We revised and expanded our college curriculum, and completed construction on our student residence and large classroom in Chénéville. The whole gang then moved north to the Wellness Center to launch our new Diploma Program.

Classes were filled to capacity and it was a joy to teach in such beautiful, natural surroundings. I loved seeing pupils gathered around the roaring bonfire on the beach at night to discuss the constellations in the star-studded sky above, or feeling the pull of a full December moon while hiking down a wintry forest trail. It was just as we had envisioned it would be.

The following summer, we built a gorgeous log chalet for our guests on the edge of the lake with a panoramic view of the water and surroundings hills. Rémi and Francis spent months hoisting, sawing and chiseling the massive timbers into shape; they reminded me of how hard my father had worked building our family home. That fall, when the lake was ablaze with the reflection of the red and gold autumn leaves, I stepped into the completed chalet and felt my father's presence all around me. The memory of standing in the tiny house he had built in the backyard for me when I was two years old came rushing back— and once again I experienced a moment of perfect happiness.

I was home, I had my palmistry family and I was living my mission.

Chénéville also became home to our extended family. Peter and Kathy's parents came to live with us when they were in their 90s and both with faltering health. They had been so good to me when I first started at the Center and it was a joy seeing them spend their final months surrounded by loving friends and family.

When they passed away, we laid them to rest in the Chénéville cemetery beneath a tall, Celtic cross. We gathered at their gravesite there, just as we had gathered years before at the Celtic cross marking Peter and Kathy's great-grandfather's grave in the foothills of the Himalayas. I marveled at how fate had brought us all (and kept us all) together, formed us into a family, bonded us to a single cause and led us to a home in a wilderness paradise.

The school was thriving and I felt a deep maternal satisfaction as many of my graduates began launching their own successful careers in palmistry as consultants and teachers. I had helped give birth to a new generation of palmists and was proud of the part I played in expanding the knowledge of *hast jyotish*. We expanded that knowledge even further when we launched a new website offering consultations and courses online to anyone on the planet with an Internet connection.

The beauty of Chénéville had crept into my heart and soul and I hated leaving it even for a weekend, but in 2013 most of the team needed to move back to Montreal for several months to focus on our classes and clients in the city. Ghanshyam, Francis and Jaysri had the task of staying in Chénéville to look after the Wellness Center in our absence, but they were too few to manage our 500-acre patch of paradise. Fortunately, one of our brightest young students, Maxime Gagnon, arrived on the scene just then and came to the rescue. Maxime had a psychology degree and a stable career in the insurance industry, but she believed in what we were doing so passionately that she quit her job and moved to Chénéville to help us keep the Wellness Center thriving.

Knowing we had such a devoted group taking care of our home allowed me to make the difficult choice to move back to the city—and maybe even saved my life.

Not long after I settled into my new apartment in Montreal, I developed severe stomach cramps and nausea. I had never suffered a serious illness before, so I figured I had just eaten too much cake the night before at Denise's birthday party. I was working from home and foolishly ignored the pain for nearly two days. Kathy dropped by for a visit and was alarmed to find me doubled over in pain and running a high fever.

"No hospitals," I groaned, clutching my belly. I had been in enough hospitals to last a lifetime.

Kathy ignored me and raced to get Peter, and as the pain was worsening by the minute, I agreed to go to the emergency room. Kathy became even more worried when I did not insist on changing out of my pajamas or putting on makeup before we left. We had been best friends for nearly 30 years and she had never seen me go out in public looking like such a mess.

"Hurry, Peter!" she urged her brother, as they helped me into his Subaru.

They got me to the hospital within five minutes, which was not a minute too soon. Apparently, my appendix had ruptured and toxins were seeping into my system and attacking my organs—causing peritonitis, a potentially fatal infection.

I barely had time to wave goodbye to Peter and Kathy before being plopped into a wheelchair, rushed into an examination room, and pumped full of antibiotics and painkillers that knocked me out.

The next morning, I was rolled into pre-op and readied for surgery. The nurse gave something to relax me and left me alone with nothing to do but stare at the big, industrial clock on the wall in front of me. Time seemed to slow down and the loud click of the clock's second hand echoed in my ears as the minutes ticked by. It was 2:45 p.m. *It would be a good time to do a Hora to see if this was an auspicious day for major surgery*, I thought. I laughed, imagining what the surgeon would say if I told him we would have to postpone the operation until the planets were more favorably aligned.

The nurse reappeared and rolled me away again. Suddenly, I was in the operating room and startled by the intensity of the lights and the number of people in the room. The anesthesiologist injected a long needle into my arm and told me to relax and breathe deeply—the same instruction I had offered countless clients who found themselves in stressful situations with uncertain outcomes.

The surgeon appeared above me, the lower part of his face covered with a green surgical mask.

"We're going to be removing your appendix today, Miss Vallée. It shouldn't take more than an hour; no need to worry, you are in good hands."

I would have liked to have seen his palms and judge for myself if I was in good hands, but his hands were gloved in latex and I was in no shape to ask anything—whatever drug I had been given was doing its job and my spirit was checking out of my body. I felt my consciousness floating upward toward the ceiling, as it had in my youth when I willed myself "into the black" to escape my troubled life. Only this time, I was not going into the black—I was going into the light.

I found myself on a battlefield among hundreds of warriors. No one had discernible facial features—we were entities of light without human form. Our bodies were comprised of vibrant, shimmering auras of fluctuating brightness, texture and color. Despite being unable to decipher shape or physical characteristics, I intuitively recognized the beautiful, radiant beings nearest to me—I was surrounded by my friends. The gang from the Center was at my side and we were engaged in a fierce battle. We did not have conventional weapons; we were armed only with the qualities we carried in our hearts—courage, truthfulness, loyalty, faith, kindness, grace and unconditional love. We were not waging war against an enemy or battling each other—we were fighting within our own selves, combating anything in our nature that was not good or was keeping us bound to ego. We were striving to become better human beings and life was our field of battle.

I have no idea how long my dream lasted, but the extensive damage my shredded appendix had wreaked on my system dragged my one-hour surgery into a complicated three-hour procedure. When the surgeon came to see me a couple of days later he told me, "You have no idea how lucky you are to be alive— we had to take your appendix out in bits and pieces, it was a real mess down there. If you hadn't gotten to the hospital when you did, we would not be having this conversation right now. It's a miracle you pulled through."

I silently thanked Maxime for joining the gang back in Chénéville—if I hadn't come to Montreal, I would not have made it to the hospital in time. I also said a prayer of thanks for Kathy and Peter— and Peter's Subaru—they had always been there when I needed them.

Immediately following the operation, I was taken to the recovery room, where I remained unconscious for two or three hours, but I knew I was not alone. Even in that deepest of sleeps, I was aware of being surrounded by a steady, repetitive musical rhythm. Then the words within the rhythm began taking shape in my mind, drawing me back to consciousness.

Om tryambakam yajāmahe sugandhim puṣti-vardhanam urvārukam-iva bandhanā mṛtyormukṣīya māmṛtāat

When I opened my eyes, I saw a beautiful circle of familiar faces hovering over me like a halo of love. Ghanshyam, Kathy, Peter, Johanne, Rémi, Francis—they were all there and chanting the Maha Mrityunjaya mantra, the ancient Vedic prayer to Lord Shiva recited to ward off untimely death and encourage healing, health and rejuvenation.

My eyes welled with tears; I was so happy to see them.

"I just came from the battlefield," I told them in a weak, hoarse whisper, and I recounted my dream. "We were all there together, we were fighting … fighting with light against darkness … I will get stronger … we will win this battle."

"I don't think it was a dream, Guylaine," Ghanshyam said. "I think you visited the astral world! Now, get some rest. You must build up your strength. We need you!"

I closed my eyes and reflected on the symbolism of my dream, or, if Ghanshyam was correct, my astral visit. The image of our team fighting together with all the goodness in our hearts will be forever locked in my memory. I was more certain than ever that I was where I was meant to be and doing the work I was meant to do.

For several days after the surgery, I was too weak even to sit up in my hospital bed and I felt so ill I worried I might not recover at all. The doctors had suggested I recuperate in the hospital for several weeks, but when a virulent intestinal bug began spreading from ward to ward, they urged me to leave immediately, fearing that in my weakened state the germ would kill me.

Peter came to get me and drove me back to my place. When we arrived, I saw he had strung up colorful Christmas lights outside my apartment to cheer me up. He helped me up the stairs, and when I opened the door, Kathy, Johanne, Denise and Rémi were there to greet me. I burst into tears—it did not matter where I was living, as long I was with such dear friends, I knew I was home.

The next several weeks were painful and frustrating. I could not do consultations and I certainly could not teach—I could barely move from one room to the other. For the first time in my life, I was forced to be still, and I spent a lot of time just sitting quietly and studying my hands—my two best friends who had never lied to me, trusted mirrors reflecting my truest self.

That reflection had altered dramatically in the three decades since I first walked into the Palmistry Center and met Ghanshyam. The entire shape of my hands had changed from conic to spatulate, revealing my transformation from an anxiety-ridden young woman lacking confidence, direction and purpose, to a committed and passionate teacher devoted to helping others and sharing the knowledge acquired after years of soul-searching and study. The worry lines that had once flecked my palms so numerously were fading or had disappeared. A Ring of Solomon had grown as I gained a better understanding of human nature and behavior and developed more empathy and compassion for others. My destiny line had become stronger as palmistry became second nature. And, most importantly to me, as I had learned to love and be loved, my once delicate heart line had grown long, strong and deep.

I had made a lot of progress, but I had so much more to learn, to accomplish and to share.

"What have you been up to?" Kathy asked, dropping in for one of her almost daily visits to check on the progress of my recovery.

"Thinking about how every hand contains an entire life story," I said.

"Well, considering you can't stand up straight yet, maybe you should start writing about that, Guylaine. This might be the perfect time to write your life story."

"No, I don't think so. I wouldn't know what to say."

"Remember what I told you before your first TV appearance? 'Let the handprints speak for themselves; each line has a story and you are there to tell that story.' Just let your hands tell the story. Think about how lost and lonely you were before you found palmistry and how it changed your life. You were miserable, and now you're a happy palmist. Your story might inspire others to follow their dreams. Just start at the beginning and write down what is most important to you."

Kathy was always a pretty smart cookie, and after she left, I thought about what she had said. It would be a while before I would be ready to go back to the classroom or do readings, so I had a lot of time on my hands. If writing about my life could inspire even one person to conquer their fears and insecurities and pursue their dreams as I had—or if I could show one person the beauty and power of palmistry—it would be well worth the effort. I would let my hands tell the story.

I opened my laptop and thought about what was most important in my life, which was simple—the two homes and the two loving families I had known, and my love of palmistry that brought them both together.

I began to type:

My first memory is a moment of perfect happiness.

Acknowledgments

All the love in my heart goes out to my mom and dad, who gave me life, unconditional love and the values I carry with me to this day. My love and thanks to my big, beautiful Vallée family—especially Réjean, Francine, Gaston, Carole, Mimi and each and every one of my nephews, nieces, grandnephews and grandnieces—I cherish and love you all!

My eternal thanks to my guru, Paramahansa Yogananda, who gave me a reason to live and the tools to lead a meaningful life. My love and thanks to my two great teachers: Ghanshyam Singh Birla, who guided me to my life's mission and has never steered me wrong; and Kathy Keogh, my BFF who taught me how to practice *hast jyotish* as a tool to help others and whose lifelong passion for palmistry has inspired me for three decades. Ghanshyam and Kathy—you live in my heart!

Thanks to all my friends at the Center, especially Peter Keogh and Johanne Riopel, who are always there for me whenever I need guidance or help, including the production of this book—I love you! My love and deepest thanks and appreciation to Denise Parisé and Rémi Riverin, my partners in this great adventure; Jaysri Côté, for her contagious spirit and optimism that inspire me every day; Francis Desjardins, who comes to my rescue in any and all emergencies; and Colette Hemlin, whose warm wishes and constant support lift me up.

A very special thank you to Hélène Dorion, our beloved poet, for her encouragement, enthusiasm and the beautiful foreword she wrote for this book.

Special thanks to beautiful Frédérique Herel, who did more than simply translate this book—she captured and reproduced the emotion and tone of Steve's wonderful English text for the French audience. It was a joy reading your work, Frédérique!

Thanks to the editing team of Johanne and Kathy, for working around the clock to complete this book, and for Johanne's revision of the French text.

Thanks to our talented artist, Philippe Couturier-Michaud, for his generosity with his computer expertise and his inspired design for the book cover.

Thanks to Pauline Edward, for her work on layout and for coordinating the publishing and to Veronica Schami for a final proofreading.

A big thanks to Maxime Gagnon, another cherished member of Team Birla, who translated original French drafts of this book into English.

A warm thanks to all the friends from years gone by who stay with me in my heart and whose love and kindness help create the memories that fill the pages of this book. And to the special friends I have been blessed to have come to know and love—I am forever grateful for your presence in my life, including Grace, Jakky, Jeannette, Nicole, Heather, Linda and Rick, Marie-Claire, Elyise, Naz, Sophie, Chandan and Émilie, and Sylvie and Jérémy. Thanks to Ghanshyam's family, Chanchala, Keero and Maryam; Rekha and Serge, and Abhish. And a warm, sunny thanks to my beautiful Miami friend Zide.

Many thanks to all my students and clients who have filled me with such joy and provided me with a sense of purpose throughout the years; each moment I have been of service to you has been a privilege and a pleasure.

Last, but not least, my greatest heartfelt thanks to my cowriter and collaborator, Steve Erwin. It is difficult to express the depth of my gratitude for his help in bringing the people I cherish to life on these pages, and for conveying the beauty of my great passions—palmistry, Kriya Yoga and meditation—in such a simple and elegant style so that (I dearly wish) many others can benefit by learning about them and, through them, find the same joy and happiness they gave me. Thanks for finding my voice and giving color to my story. You and your beautiful wife, Natasha, are truly miracles in my life.

—Guylaine Vallée

Guylaine, thank you for entrusting me with your story—like you, it is beautiful through and through. Working with you has stretched my heart; your friendship means the world to me.

A huge thank you to the entire gang at the Center; to Kathy and Johanne, for shepherding the book with patience, diligence and tender care; to Peter, for the confounding swimming hole philosophy; to Jaysri, Denise, Rémi, Francis and Maxime, for inviting me into your homes and lives and making me feel so loved—the feeling is mutual. And biggest thanks to Ghanshyam, for providing a universe where stars shine so brightly—you are a mentor of love and I am blessed to call you friend.

And to my wife, Natasha, thank you for pushing me to always do better, for your forbearance and love, and for putting up with me for 20 years. You are my North Star.

—Steve Erwin

About the Authors

Guylaine Vallée grew up in the small town of Valleyfield, Quebec and graduated from the television program at Cégep de Jonquière's School of Media Arts and Technology. She had a successful career as a scriptwriter and film editor in Paris and Montreal, but left the television industry after meeting world-renowned palmist Ghanshyam Singh Birla. Her life was so transformed by the ancient science of Vedic palmistry that she dedicated her life to its study and practice. In her 30 years as a professional palmist she has helped thousands of clients improve their lives and has inspired tens of thousands lecturing across North America and through her many radio and television appearances. Guylaine lives and practices palmistry in Montreal and Chénéville, Quebec.

Steve Erwin, a Toronto-born writer and award-winning journalist, has worked in print and broadcast media for 25 years in Canada and the United States. In New York City, he was a Foreign Correspondent for the Canadian Broadcasting Corporation, reporting on the 9/11 tragedy and its aftermath, and a national news and feature writer for *People* magazine. He has written seven books, including *The New York Times* best-selling memoir *Left to Tell: Discovering God Amidst the Rwandan Holocaust* with Immaculée Ilibagiza, which has sold more than 1 million copies and has been translated into more than 20 languages. He divides his time between Manhattan, Ontario and the Outaouais region of Quebec with his wife, journalist and author Natasha Stoynoff.

For Further Reading

The River of Life: 90-Day Interactive Journal
Kathleen E. Keogh and Guylaine Vallée

The River of Life is an interactive 90-day journal of self-discovery and a highly effective tool for personal growth and positive change. It is based on the principle of Vedic palmistry that once we begin making positive life changes, it takes 90 days for those inner changes to be reflected in the lines and signs of our hand. This powerful little book is meant to accompany and encourage you on your journey of positive transformation. Each page features an inspirational quote, a space to record your thoughts and a self-awareness chart to help you recognize and understand your daily energy level and behavior patterns through the Ayurvedic theory of *tridoshas*—the balance of elements within our bodies.

When used every day, *The River of Life* journal helps you navigate the currents of your life, turn negative traits and situations into positive ones, and transform obstacles, anxiety and doubt into opportunities, insight and inspiration.

Introduction to Hast Jyotish: Ancient Eastern System of Palmistry

Ghanshyam Singh Birla

"The Introduction to Hast Jyotish textbook is a significant, authentic and masterly contribution to the study of the ancient Indian system of palmistry."
—Dr. Vasant Lad, Ayurvedic Physician, Founder of the Ayurvedic Institute

Introduction to Hast Jyotish is a must-read for anyone interested in the history, philosophy and practice of Vedic palmistry. This fascinating and fastidiously researched study of the ancient science of Vedic palmistry is both an indispensable guide for the student of *hast jyotish* and a valuable reference book for every professional palmist. Renowned astro-palmist Ghanshyam Singh Birla distills 50 years of experience and practice into this compact yet comprehensive masterpiece. It provides a systematic approach to the rich and complex subject of Vedic palmistry and is also a thoroughly entertaining read. Topics include:

- The principles of *hast jyotish* within the Vedic tradition
- The historical roots of palmistry in world cultures
- The geography of the hand
- Hand types: different paths to personal growth
- The fingers: our conscious expression
- The thumb: indicator of our individuality
- The nails: armor of our nervous system
- Exploring our three levels of consciousness through the hand—the mounts (superconscious); the major lines (subconscious); the minor lines (conscious)
- Tracing our evolutionary/Karmic progress through the hands

Introduction au hast jyotish : Système ancestral de chirologie védique is the French version of this book by Ghanshyam Singh Birla and Guylaine Vallée.

Contact the Author

Guylaine Vallée is available for consultations, coaching, lectures, media events and workshops.

To know more about Guylaine's services, upcoming events and publications, visit her Facebook page and her website (www.guylainevallee.com) or contact the Birla Center toll-free at 514-488-2292 or 1-866-428-3799.

For more information on online palmistry courses, visit Birla College at www.birla.ca/college. You can register online in our secure boutique.

The Birla College is fully recognized by both the Quebec provincial Government

Courses taken by residents of Canada are eligible for tax credits.

Online Palmistry Courses with Guylaine Vallée

Introduction to Hast Jyotish

This course is the first step for anyone who wants to learn more about themselves or those contemplating a career as a consultant in Vedic palmistry.

Adventure in Consciousness: Exploring the Astrological Zones of the Hand

The mounts, the astrological zones of the hand, relate to our innermost self, which forms the core of our being. In essence, they reveal who we truly are. Learn all the tests used to determine the level of mount formation.

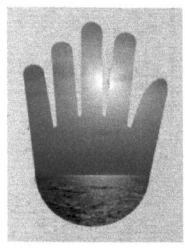

Moon: Perception, Emotions and Creativity

All the information we receive about the world around us is filtered through Luna. When Luna is balanced, we choose to see our personal future in an optimistic light and the world as a beautiful place.

Venus: Feeling Good in Your Body

Venus can reveal our potential to love and be loved, and to be filled with the joy of being alive. It is also the seat of our physical needs, longings, wants and desires.

Mars Galaxy: Living in Stress or Harmony?

Mars Negative relates to our physical energy, while Mars Positive focuses on our mental attributes. They work together just as a long-distance runner needs both the physical energy as well as the mental stamina to run a successful marathon and reach the finish line.

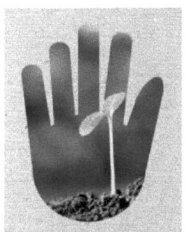

Jupiter: Deciphering our Life Purpose

Jupiter, referred to as the Guru, translates literally as "dispeller of darkness", motivating us to seek the meaning of existence and find our purpose.

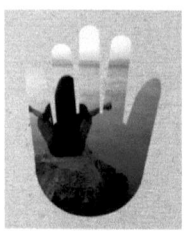

Saturn: A Potent Force for Change

Saturn is the mount of transformation and, as fire transforms iron into steel, Saturn energy can turn the challenges, pain, hardship and suffering we experience in life into awareness, wisdom, strength of character, and compassion for others.

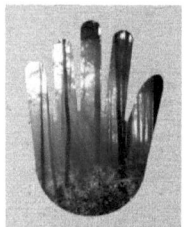

Sun: Attracting Your Heart's Desires

The mount and finger of the Sun represent our direct connection to our own heart and feelings of universal love. Just as the physical Sun is a radiating body of unimaginable light and heat, the force of our personal Sun can radiate a strength and magnetism to realize our dreams.

Mercury: The Art of Communication

According to Western mythology, Mercury (or Hermes) is the messenger of the gods. Similarly, in our hands, the mount of Mercury reflects our ability to communicate ideas clearly and effortlessly.

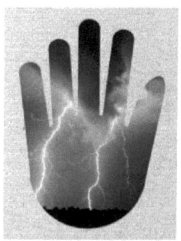

Rahu and Ketu: Understanding Your Karmic Mission

A famous Sanskrit verse tells us that, "our present is the result of all our yesterdays, and the future depends on how well we live today." This sums up the relationship between Ketu, representing the kinds of circumstances we attracted in the past, and Rahu, representing our present circumstances with a vision for the future.

The Heart Line: The Secrets of Love

The Heart Line is a window into our soul and plays a tremendous role in revealing whom we choose to love, why, and what kind of people choose to love us.

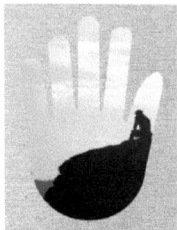

The Head Line: Moral Compass

The mind can be both a powerful tool for seeking truth, self-awareness and spiritual enlightenment, but it can also distort our perception of reality, causing us to place limits on our growth and misjudge and mistreat others by jumping to incorrect conclusions.

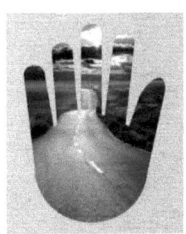

The Life Line: Physical Health and Well-Being

The Life Line provides us with invaluable information about our physical wellbeing. Depending on its formation, the life line provides a strong physical foundation of support for our thoughts (Head Line) and feelings (Heart Line).

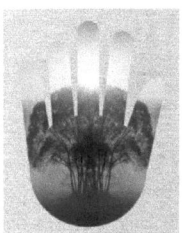

The Line of Saturn: Achieving our Life Purpose

Understanding your Saturn or destiny line helps reveal your talents, potentials and any hurdles you might have in realizing your life's purpose and karmic mission.

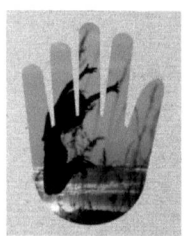

The Sun line: Attracting Happiness and Success

This course is about understanding your Sun Line as a gauge of magnetism in drawing success and love into your life.

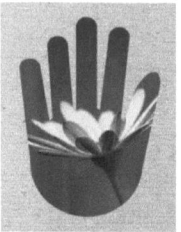

The Line of Mercury: Communication, Intuition and Enlightenment

This course enables you to understand all facets of your Mercury Line in order to express with greater ease and eloquence in all circumstances.

The Girdle of Venus: Emotional Balance & Creativity

The study of the Girdle of Venus reveals how your attitude is helping or hindering the process of tapping into your inner joy and steps you can take to express your feelings more creatively.

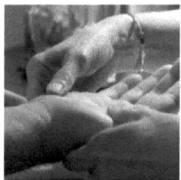

Consultant in Training: Diagnosis, Interpretation and Delivery

This course will help you recognize and interpret specific aspects of the hand, in order to combine them for an overall analysis.

Printed by Libri Plureos GmbH in Hamburg, Germany